# A System for Survival
## GIS and Sustainable Development

**Allan Falconer and
Joyce Foresman, editors**

*with contributions from*
Basanta Shrestha, Birendra Bajracharya, Sushil
Pradhan, and Timothy W. Foresman

ESRI PRESS
REDLANDS, CALIFORNIA

#51/0290

ESRI
  A System for Survival: GIS and Sustainable Development
  ISBN 1-58948-052-X

First printing July 2002.

Printed in the United States of America.

Published by ESRI, 380 New York Street, Redlands, California 92373-8100.

Books from ESRI Press are available to resellers worldwide through Independent Publishers Group (IPG). For information on volume discounts, or to place an order, call IPG at 1-800-888-4741 in the United States, or at 312-337-0747 outside the United States.

# CONTENTS

# ACKNOWLEDGMENTS

We would like to extend our thanks to the following organizations and individuals for their encouragement, support, and contributions without which this book would not exist:

Earth Charter, Earth Council

International Center for Remote Sensing Education, Baltimore, Maryland

Basanta Shrestha, Birendra Bajracharya, and Sushil Pradhan of the International Centre for Integrated Mountain Development, authors of *GIS for Beginners*

United Nations Environmental Programme

David Smith, U.S. Department of State

Andrej Loncaric at GISDATA

Pedro Barrero, Omar Baleani, and Adrian Benitez at Aeroterra S.A.

Jason Rohweder at United States Geological Survey

Fire Captain Specialist Tim Walsh at Marin County Fire Department

Nancy Tosta, Ross & Associates Environmental Consulting, Ltd.

# INTRODUCTION

## SUSTAINABLE DEVELOPMENT AND GEOGRAPHIC INFORMATION SYSTEMS

*Allan Falconer*
University of Mississippi and Mississippi Space Commerce Initiative

We have in recent years begun to view our planet as an oasis in the universe, or as Buckminster Fuller described it "our spaceship earth." This realization, that the planet is virtually a closed system with finite resources, is a salutary one. Overtaxing its resources, or fouling the nest, will destroy our ability to live on it. Current observations indicate that this is beginning to occur. Both terrestrial and marine species are being depleted at an alarming rate. Species extinction results in the reduction of animal and plant diversity—ramifications of which can be felt in every strand of the complex web of life—and, in many cases, the total populations of surviving species are being reduced also. The human population of the earth continues to grow exponentially as well, and the frustrating irony is that the very activities we engage in to make our civilization viable is the means of its destruction.

The concept of "sustainable development" is therefore intuitively attractive: it suggests the possibility that certain types of development may continue indefinitely. Such a possibility has nearly as much appeal as the idea of perpetual motion or even the philosopher's stone. Sustainable development has consequently become something of a buzzword for a vague panacea. To the environmentalist it means neutral development, or *no damage to the trees, flowers, or creatures*; to the developer it means continuous cash flow, because *our developments have had a positive impact on thousands of families and businesses in the area*; while to most of us it means developments that *don't cause real damage or cost much—we can continue to increase our standard of living without worrying about running out of resources or hurting the planet.*

In the midst of all this headlong human activity, we are nevertheless becoming conscious of a need to be more prudent and far-seeing in the management of our lives. If the days of growing vegetables in the family garden are in fact gone, we are recognizing the value of local farmers' markets and organic produce; and instead of burying our tin cans and bottles in pits in our backyards, we support comprehensive recycling programs. If we no longer have unexplored continents to which we might export our problems and import our necessities and luxuries, we are beginning to grasp the possibilities in our new technologies: energy from the wind and the sun and the tides.

And yet there is a paradox at work here, too. We are now consuming the resources we seek to protect in the process of protecting them. It's not much of an exaggeration to think of the trees that are felled and milled just to provide forest managers with paper to promote better forest management. The aim of better management, generally speaking, is to get more from less; environmentally, that means using in ways that do not run our resources dry, ways that allow us to live well but not at the expense of generations to come. We cannot, for example, look at streams and rivers being managed as part of vast and complicated hydro projects that conserve water, generate electricity, and provide irrigation—and not consider the severe consequences of those benefits: degradation of the health of a particular floodplain or riverine ecosystem.

Is the problem one of management? Are we simply poor managers? We have in any case a situation in which self-protection has become the paramount need, and justification by data (or process) the technique of choice. The provision of data for this purpose has spawned the ballyhooed Information Age. Here again is an intuitive attraction: what could possibly be wrong with more and more information? Information has infinite potential because it is inherently inexhaustible. Consider, however, the online video camera observing nonevents in a convenience store twenty-four hours a day, seven days a week. Every bit, byte, and pixel is information of some type, but its value is transitory and questionable, if not altogether illusory.

Our efforts then need to focus on the generation and analysis of information that has value, and that information needs to be communicated to those who can use it. The practice of hoarding information in order to exert control, generate wealth, or more efficiently extort value from the resources is now widely developed and often admired. Practitioners of this art have become adept at doing nothing but simply presenting the facts. They become default data-czars because they control information, and cannot be impeached because by doing nothing, they do nothing wrong!

This means that our most valuable resources, people who can "do, teach, and manage" act only in response or reaction to those who do nothing. Facts are introduced into the arena of concern, and are duly classified, filed, and held until their value is recognized. We are currently at the mercy of a process of random recognition where a "fact" or a data set is not necessarily tied to any defined policy or belief system that might protect our future. Consequently, the impact of development can only be understood when the cumulative impact of many decisions is recorded, mapped, and monitored. These activities occur in the zone of interaction between remote sensing, geographic information systems (GIS), and the global positioning system (GPS). Geospatial technology (the inclusive term) provides a remarkable opportunity to understand the nature of our impact on this planet's natural system. In fact, some adherents would argue that the proactive application of these technologies represent humankind's last best chance to solve the critical problems facing "earthians" to borrow another Fuller term.

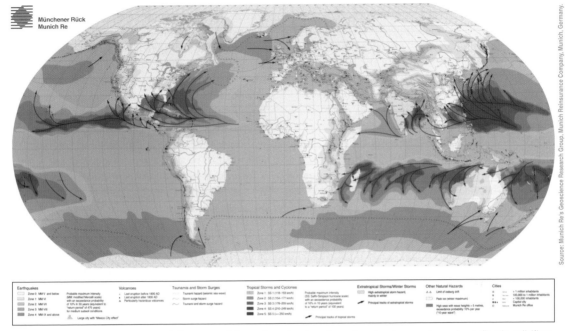

This "World Map of Natural Hazards" presents information about earthquakes, hurricanes, tornadoes, floods, wildfires, lightning strikes, and numerous other natural phenomena. It was made using satellite imagery, risk analysis outcomes, and other sources of data, and demonstrates both the inclusiveness and reach of geographic information systems—especially their ability to measure the world in great detail, and synthesize vast amounts of information.

Whatever we do as we struggle to sustainably develop our world, we must understand that the geographical concept of scale will apply in both time and space. Geographical dimensions of location change over time, and the time scale is important if we consider how we are to view sustainability. If it is in terms of a human life span then we need to consider days and decades and generations. If it is in terms of political action then we need to consider political time in election cycles (two, four, six, year terms at the U.S. national level and various combinations at the local level). Neither of these scales relate to geological time in a meaningful way. Nor do they relate well to natural cycles in weather patterns and the closely linked hydrological events such as the flood events for a river regime.

The concept of sustainable development therefore hangs on vague and opportunistically flexible notions—if they are not altogether illusions—of "time" and "resources." The utility of a resource and its sustainability is a function of time and technology, geography and science. Current technology relies heavily upon electricity, and therefore on oil, coal, water, wind, and nuclear energy. Only wind and water were of any interest as a "resource" until the Industrial Revolution, and now they are only of indirect value to information technology as a source of electricity. Geographers have for many centuries understood that the value of a commodity is a function of its location. Hence the distribution of a resource determines its utility and so relates to its economic value. A simple example of water as a resource captures these concepts. For many centuries, human life was centered around water and any settlement typically associated itself with a water supply. Desert regions provided a major focus for this and the concept of an oasis defined an early stage in the concept of sustainable development. Overtaxing the water supply or poisoning it destroyed the oasis. Abandoned oases in desert regions speak persuasively of these events.

If the human species is to survive, we must first make a firmly conclusive distinction—not a choice—between survival of current lives and survival of lives yet to come. We need to manage the resources necessary to sustain the entire spectrum of human—and by logical extension, plant and animal—life. Therefore, it is important that we have information about the location, quantity, and quality of those resources. Proper management requires information about the rates of use and the rates of change of resources, and availability of alternate resources. Changing technology will determine the amount of resources that will need to be converted to human use. With information referenced accurately by location we can assess the problem and make appropriate management decisions.

In recent years, three technologies have evolved to assist our management of the diverse data of time and space: remote sensing, GPS, and GIS. Remote sensing technology allows us to survey the whole earth with unprecedented regularity. Systems developed by NASA provide extraordinarily detailed images—resolutions from one to thirty meters—of nearly 80 percent of Earth's land mass, and weather satellites monitor cloud systems and global atmospheric conditions every hour. Using these views from space we can see droughts, floods, and fires in a regional perspective. These information resources are unprecedented and give us the ability to compile current inventories of urban sprawl, damage by forest fires, other natural disasters including floods, assessments of vegetation vigor (several times each growing season), and many other inventories of natural resources.

GIS provides the tools to accurately map this information in both global and local terms. Georeferencing—the process of identifying the precise location of a feature on the earth's surface—can be done with a GPS receiver that will read satellite signals and calculate the precise earth coordinates of its location. Fully georeferenced data can then be managed, analyzed, and mapped in a GIS. Georeferenced remote sensing data is equally suited to such treatment, becoming in the process virtual orthophotos of the earth's surface.

With information that records the location of many different properties of the earth, it becomes possible to use a GIS to relate vegetation cover to infrastructure. This allows a crew chief at a forest fire, for example, to use GPS data from aircraft or helicopters to map the fire boundary and to use the GIS to show where the power lines are in the burning area. He can have power switched off to prevent problems. Also, using the infrastructure information he can do the same with gas and water pipelines and plan the safest road access to valve locations or pumping stations. The flexibility of the GIS makes it possible for the chief to include a vegetation map in his strategic and tactical planning and estimate the probable burn of the fire for each of several possible changes in the wind.

The emergency situation of a fire or flood suggests entirely laudable but short-term use of the system. Over a longer period of time the same system allows the comparison of natural resources at different dates and thus the calculation of rates of change or consumption. Information about roads, rail tracks, canals, power transmission corridors, and the network services (water, natural gas, electricity, telephone, cable) can be supplied to residential customers. Using this information as a resource, managers and users together have an unprecedented ability to study the links between natural resources and economic infrastructure.

---

Recent advances in commercial remote sensing systems have seen the marketing of data with 1.0 meter and 0.62 meter resolution. Both these systems use satellites, meaning we have the real possibility of examining our global village at scales from the local to the continental (approximately 1:10,000 through 1:8,000,000). With adequate computer capacity this can be done using a zoom capacity with a location accuracy of better than 10 meters, depending on scale.

Such systems offer the typical manager of resources incalculable benefits—if the data can be accessed in a timely manner and the information extracted efficiently. The brief examples that follow in this book illustrate how GIS technology has already provided managers with insight and the ability to act and react in a way simply not possible before. The many scales of resource study and development represented in these studies range from the successful use of GIS to plot the plumes of lethal chlorine gas spilling from a train wreck in Montana through the monitoring of the rate of tropical forest depletion in Madagascar to a depiction of the effects of El Niño ocean warming.

More detailed studies can reveal the dynamics of change in food crops as the growing season progresses. This is a vital component in assessing the need for famine relief and the monitoring of drought. Other uses of vegetation monitoring include the modeling and prediction of recovery rates after a drought or flood. Such work requires the detailed knowledge of soils, erosion rates, nutrient cycles, and the local agricultural practices. If properly integrated with weather data, these models can contribute to the understanding of river regimes and to the better management of water resources—which makes for better management of resources in the event of an emergency, natural or man-made.

There is great efficiency in using remote sensing data as layers or coverages in a GIS. The availability of tabular data in the GIS that can be associated with the remote sensing images is a functional benefit further enhanced by the other layers of map data that permit the manager to view the occurrence of image features in relation to geological boundaries, vegetation zones, or any earth science information. When these features are viewed in conjunction with population data and socio-economic data, the result is often an improved understanding of the roots of conflict or the basis for the resolution of disputes.

The efficient use of a GIS provides for a better understanding of environmental issues also. The mapping of a habitat and its inclusion in the GIS may reveal the nature of conflict between wildlife and human populations. Conservation issues and the animal population data relating to livestock and wildlife are often related to socio-economic infrastructure. Habitat characteristics can be added to these using GIS techniques. The essential functions of a geographical analysis can be exercised and related to decision support requirements for management. Managers can use this to build models of systems and then use the models to assess the impact of each of a series of potential decisions. These modeled responses can be taken together to assess the cumulative effects of a series of management decisions so that the outcome can be finely tuned before decisions become irrevocable.

It is doubtful that we will ever have perfect models available for our research and planning, and it is apparent that sustainability is a function of many factors; no single factor or group of factors will adequately define sustainability, however spectacular our models become. But as each element of these models is improved, our ability to provide realistic outcomes for the guidance of managers increases demonstrably and substantially. It is the geographic impact of cumulative decisions in a specific region that determines the sustainability of the region, and it is therefore important to make those decisions according to both individual components of an ecosystem, region, or local area, and the sum of their interactivity. The scope called for in such decisions is realistic only if vast amounts of information can be made readily available, easy to handle, and—lest we forget the need for participation of the broadest, most inclusive sort—conducive to display and communication.

---

The concepts of sustainability in the full geographic context are captured in The Earth Charter. In 1987, the United Nations World Commission on Environment and Development called for a new charter setting forth the principles for sustainable development. The Rio Earth Summit of 1992 left this as a piece of unfinished business and in 1994 Maurice Strong, Chairman of the Earth Council and Secretary General of the Earth Summit, and Mikhail Gorbachev, President of Green Cross International, launched a new Earth Charter initiative with support from the Dutch Government. An Earth Charter Commission was formed in 1997 to oversee the project.

The Earth Charter, approved by the Commission at a meeting in UNESCO headquarters in Paris in 2000, has four major principles, including respect and care for the community of life; ecological integrity; social and economic justice; and democracy, nonviolence, and peace. Each of these principles has four components. Central to this charter is the definition of "sustainable" and the steps that can be taken to firmly link this to development.

All these elements are involved in our existence. The Earth Charter captures and addresses each dimension in its four main principles. The striking thing is that in order to understand how each element impacts each of us we need to know the location of the problems, the resources, and the solutions. We also need to know the areas where there are no problems so that we can appreciate what gives us problem-free development. This knowledge of location gives us the geography of the situation and relates us each to the other as we see how our global village is structured.

The technology of geographical information systems (GIS) is described at the end of this book. The brilliant encapsulation of the technology is a contribution from the International Centre for Integrated Mountain Development (ICIMOD) and is reprinted here by permission. Before we can look at the use of this technology in sustainable development we need to understand the broad context of world development and the importance of preserving those elements that are essential for continued human existence on this planet.

## VALUE SYSTEMS AND THE CONCEPT OF SUSTAINABLE DEVELOPMENT

A practical understanding of sustainable development—as opposed to one in which it is all things to all people—clearly depends upon the negotiation and acceptance of a value system. The Earth Charter's concluding remarks, "The Way Forward," speaks eloquently and persuasively of this precondition. Here the emphasis is on abiding values—not temporary or illusory needs—and the desire for our society "to be remembered for the awakening of a new reverence for life, the firm resolve to achieve sustainability, the quickening of the struggle for justice and peace, and the joyful celebration of life." These desires are visible universally in the human desire to live joyfully and to celebrate the planet where we are privileged to live out our lives.

Millenia have passed, but we are slowly realizing the futility of enslaving each other. We are becoming, as well, more receptive to the idea that enslaving ourselves in the pursuit of power is a dead end. Similarly, our wish to own the resources of the world has come to seem a futile pursuit. No matter if the desire is to corner the market in silver, or pork bellies, or timber, or sand; there are few indications that this kind of success produces a joyful celebration of life.

Certain freedoms seem to appeal to us individually, and to be more conducive to the common good when we act collectively. The distinguishing of, and search for, these freedoms requires a reverence for human life and a wish for a society that provides above all for peace and security. None of us asked to be born and so we are "all in this together." Notions of sustainability and peaceful coexistence inhere in each other. The earth can, in fact, sustain civilized human life, and has done so for several thousands of years. However, the mechanisms of sustainability must be understood and the balance between the various elements of our existence must be translated into operational requirements: air that is fit to breathe, water that is fit to drink, food that is fit to eat, and shelter free of threats both from within and without.

These fundamentals permeate all aspects of sustainability. But even the basic requirement of air that is fit to breathe is not guaranteed to all. In Bhopal, India, in 1984, when escaping gases from a chemical factory poisoned the air and caused the death of thousands, we saw a dramatic illustration of the failure to sustain air quality at a level required for human life. We see this on a daily basis as well on industrial farms where chickens, cattle, or swine are kept in large numbers to efficiently and profitably produce food, and where the effluent results in local air pollution. Similar effects are found in a variety of industries processing chemicals. Although the discussion is of air being fit for humans to breathe, these stories revolve around food production and chemical processing, both of which are inextricably linked to our existence.

The manufacturing of fertilizer, herbicides, pesticides, and food packaging, and the refining of the petroleum necessary to mechanized farming, are all activities that may pollute the air and water at the same time they play important roles in the complicated processes of supplying food to billions of people. How much pollution can be tolerated in a food production cycle before basic air and water needs are compromised to the point where they are no longer viable is yet to be determined. What is clear, however, in all cases, is that there is a growing need to measure the impact of these activities. These measurements are better understood if they are mapped because we may then understand the consequences geographically—that is to say, we can see where, and to whom, these consequences are occurring. We can see directions and rates of change and therefore make more reliable predictions of directions and rates of change to come.

GIS is being used to generate and support these cartographic inquiries, and the examples given here are an illustration of the new kind of work that geographers are doing and will do, as well as the power of the new tools they can employ. Sustainability is a story of incredibly complicated connections, and GIS is a story of clear juxtapositions of complicated connections. Consider this: Just as the simple concept of food production becomes inextricably linked to air and water quality, it is linked just as inextricably to issues of peace and security, as food production is

typically reduced or inhibited or altogether shut down in war zones and areas of civil unrest. A single map would become a rather cluttered and unreadable—ineffective and unusable—affair if it tried to illustrate all the information underlying these forces and consequences. The right kind of GIS makes this kind of analysis a matter of course.

If all human societies are to share in the joy of life then these issues must be addressed. If life is to be celebrated we must devise inclusive strategies, and socioeconomic practices must be adopted that both reflect changing technologies and accommodate human rights. By constantly reviewing the global situation, in other words by paying constant attention to our geography, we can increase our understanding of the complexities of the one planet that can support our existence.

Indeed, if we base our actions upon our understanding we may achieve the necessary sustainability in the systems essential for human life. The themes discussed here are an attempt to illustrate this.

*Bibliography*

Cooke, Ronald U., and James H. Johnson, eds. 1969. *Trends in Geography: An Introductory Survey*. London: Pergamon Press.

Dotto, Lydia. 1986. *Planet Earth in Jeopardy: Environmental Consequences of Nuclear War*. Chichester, UK: John Wiley and Sons.

Prah, Kwesi K., ed. 1987. *Food Security Issues in Southern Africa*. Maseru: Institute of Southern African Studies, University of Lesotho.

Renner, Michael. 1993. *Critical Juncture: The Future of Peace Keeping*. Washington, D.C.: Worldwatch Institute.

Sakharov, Andrei D. 1968. *Progress, Coexistence & Intellectual Freedom*. New York: W. W. Norton & Company, Inc.

# THE EARTH CHARTER

The Earth Charter is an authoritative synthesis of values, principles, and aspirations that are widely shared by growing numbers of men and women in all regions of the world. The principles of the Earth Charter reflect extensive international consultations conducted over a period of many years. These principles are also based upon contemporary science, international law, and the insights of philosophy and religion. Successive drafts of the Earth Charter were circulated around the world for comment and debate by nongovernmental organizations, community groups, professional societies, and international experts in many fields.

For more information about the Earth Charter and its endorsement status, visit *www.earthcharter.org.*

## PREAMBLE

We stand at a critical moment in Earth's history, a time when humanity must choose its future. As the world becomes increasingly interdependent and fragile, the future at once holds great peril and great promise. To move forward we must recognize that in the midst of a magnificent diversity of cultures and life forms we are one human family and one Earth community with a common destiny. We must join together to bring forth a sustainable global society founded on respect for nature, universal human rights, economic justice, and a culture of peace. Towards this end, it is imperative that we, the peoples of Earth, declare our responsibility to one another, to the greater community of life, and to future generations.

*Earth, our home*
Humanity is part of a vast evolving universe. Earth, our home, is alive with a unique community of life. The forces of nature make existence a demanding and uncertain adventure, but Earth has provided the conditions essential to life's evolution. The resilience of the community of life and the well-being of humanity depend upon preserving a healthy biosphere with all its ecological systems, a rich variety of plants and animals, fertile soils, pure waters, and clean air. The global environment with its finite resources is a common concern of all peoples. The protection of Earth's vitality, diversity, and beauty is a sacred trust.

*The global situation*

The dominant patterns of production and consumption are causing environmental devastation, the depletion of resources, and a massive extinction of species. Communities are being undermined. The benefits of development are not shared equitably and the gap between rich and poor is widening. Injustice, poverty, ignorance, and violent conflict are widespread and the cause of great suffering. An unprecedented rise in human population has overburdened ecological and social systems. The foundations of global security are threatened. These trends are perilous—but not inevitable.

*The challenges ahead*

The choice is ours: form a global partnership to care for Earth and one another or risk the destruction of ourselves and the diversity of life. Fundamental changes are needed in our values, institutions, and ways of living. We must realize that when basic needs have been met, human development is primarily about being more, not having more. We have the knowledge and technology to provide for all and to reduce our impacts on the environment. The emergence of a global civil society is creating new opportunities to build a democratic and humane world. Our environmental, economic, political, social, and spiritual challenges are interconnected, and together we can forge inclusive solutions.

*Universal responsibility*

To realize these aspirations, we must decide to live with a sense of universal responsibility, identifying ourselves with the whole Earth community as well as our local communities. We are at once citizens of different nations and of one world in which the local and global are linked. Everyone shares responsibility for the present and future well-being of the human family and the larger living world. The spirit of human solidarity and kinship with all life is strengthened when we live with reverence for the mystery of being, gratitude for the gift of life, and humility regarding the human place in nature.

We urgently need a shared vision of basic values to provide an ethical foundation for the emerging world community. Therefore, together in hope we affirm the following interdependent principles for a sustainable way of life as a common standard by which the conduct of all individuals, organizations, businesses, governments, and transnational institutions is to be guided and assessed.

# PRINCIPLES

*I. Respect and care for the community of life*

**1** *Respect Earth and life in all its diversity.*
  **a** Recognize that all beings are interdependent and every form of life has value regardless of its worth to human beings.
  **b** Affirm faith in the inherent dignity of all human beings and in the intellectual, artistic, ethical, and spiritual potential of humanity.

**2** *Care for the community of life with understanding, compassion, and love.*
  **a** Accept that with the right to own, manage, and use natural resources comes the duty to prevent environmental harm and to protect the rights of people.
  **b** Affirm that with increased freedom, knowledge, and power comes increased responsibility to promote the common good.

**3** *Build democratic societies that are just, participatory, sustainable, and peaceful.*
  **a** Ensure that communities at all levels guarantee human rights and fundamental freedoms and provide everyone an opportunity to realize his or her full potential.
  **b** Promote social and economic justice, enabling all to achieve a secure and meaningful livelihood that is ecologically responsible.

**4** *Secure Earth's bounty and beauty for present and future generations.*
  **a** Recognize that the freedom of action of each generation is qualified by the needs of future generations.
  **b** Transmit to future generations values, traditions, and institutions that support the long-term flourishing of Earth's human and ecological communities.

In order to fulfill these four broad commitments, it is necessary to:

*II. Ecological integrity*

**5** *Protect and restore the integrity of Earth's ecological systems, with special concern for biological diversity and the natural processes that sustain life.*
  **a** Adopt at all levels sustainable development plans and regulations that make environmental conservation and rehabilitation integral to all development initiatives.
  **b** Establish and safeguard viable nature and biosphere reserves, including wild lands and marine areas, to protect Earth's life support systems, maintain biodiversity, and preserve our natural heritage.
  **c** Promote the recovery of endangered species and ecosystems.
  **d** Control and eradicate non-native or genetically modified organisms harmful to native species and the environment, and prevent introduction of such harmful organisms.
  **e** Manage the use of renewable resources such as water, soil, forest products, and marine life in ways that do not exceed rates of regeneration and that protect the health of ecosystems.
  **f** Manage the extraction and use of non-renewable resources such as minerals and fossil fuels in ways that minimize depletion and cause no serious environmental damage.

**6** *Prevent harm as the best method of environmental protection and, when knowledge is limited, apply a precautionary approach.*

   **a** Take action to avoid the possibility of serious or irreversible environmental harm even when scientific knowledge is incomplete or inconclusive.

   **b** Place the burden of proof on those who argue that a proposed activity will not cause significant harm, and make the responsible parties liable for environmental harm.

   **c** Ensure that decision making addresses the cumulative, long-term, indirect, long distance, and global consequences of human activities.

   **d** Prevent pollution of any part of the environment and allow no build-up of radioactive, toxic, or other hazardous substances.

   **e** Avoid military activities damaging to the environment.

**7** *Adopt patterns of production, consumption, and reproduction that safeguard Earth's regenerative capacities, human rights, and community well-being.*

   **a** Reduce, reuse, and recycle the materials used in production and consumption systems, and ensure that residual waste can be assimilated by ecological systems.

   **b** Act with restraint and efficiency when using energy, and rely increasingly on renewable energy sources such as solar and wind.

   **c** Promote the development, adoption, and equitable transfer of environmentally sound technologies.

   **d** Internalize the full environmental and social costs of goods and services in the selling price, and enable consumers to identify products that meet the highest social and environmental standards.

   **e** Ensure universal access to health care that fosters reproductive health and responsible reproduction.

   **f** Adopt lifestyles that emphasize the quality of life and material sufficiency in a finite world.

**8** *Advance the study of ecological sustainability and promote the open exchange and wide application of the knowledge acquired.*

   **a** Support international scientific and technical cooperation on sustainability, with special attention to the needs of developing nations.

   **b** Recognize and preserve the traditional knowledge and spiritual wisdom in all cultures that contribute to environmental protection and human well-being.

   **c** Ensure that information of vital importance to human health and environmental protection, including genetic information, remains available in the public domain.

*III. Social and economic justice*

9 *Eradicate poverty as an ethical, social, and environmental imperative.*
   a Guarantee the right to potable water, clean air, food security, uncontaminated soil, shelter, and safe sanitation, allocating the national and international resources required.
   b Empower every human being with the education and resources to secure a sustainable livelihood, and provide social security and safety nets for those who are unable to support themselves.
   c Recognize the ignored, protect the vulnerable, serve those who suffer, and enable them to develop their capacities and to pursue their aspirations.

10 *Ensure that economic activities and institutions at all levels promote human development in an equitable and sustainable manner.*
   a Promote the equitable distribution of wealth within nations and among nations.
   b Enhance the intellectual, financial, technical, and social resources of developing nations, and relieve them of onerous international debt.
   c Ensure that all trade supports sustainable resource use, environmental protection, and progressive labor standards.
   d Require multinational corporations and international financial organizations to act transparently in the public good, and hold them accountable for the consequences of their activities.

11 *Affirm gender equality and equity as prerequisites to sustainable development and ensure universal access to education, health care, and economic opportunity.*
   a Secure the human rights of women and girls and end all violence against them.
   b Promote the active participation of women in all aspects of economic, political, civil, social, and cultural life as full and equal partners, decision makers, leaders, and beneficiaries.
   c Strengthen families and ensure the safety and loving nurture of all family members.

12 *Uphold the right of all, without discrimination, to a natural and social environment supportive of human dignity, bodily health, and spiritual well-being, with special attention to the rights of indigenous peoples and minorities.*
   a Eliminate discrimination in all its forms, such as that based on race, color, sex, sexual orientation, religion, language, and national, ethnic or social origin.
   b Affirm the right of indigenous peoples to their spirituality, knowledge, lands and resources and to their related practice of sustainable livelihoods.
   c Honor and support the young people of our communities, enabling them to fulfill their essential role in creating sustainable societies.
   d Protect and restore outstanding places of cultural and spiritual significance.

*IV. Democracy, nonviolence, and peace*

**13** *Strengthen democratic institutions at all levels, and provide transparency and accountability in governance, inclusive participation in decision making, and access to justice.*
   a Uphold the right of everyone to receive clear and timely information on environmental matters and all development plans and activities which are likely to affect them or in which they have an interest.
   b Support local, regional and global civil society, and promote the meaningful participation of all interested individuals and organizations in decision making.
   c Protect the rights to freedom of opinion, expression, peaceful assembly, association, and dissent.
   d Institute effective and efficient access to administrative and independent judicial procedures, including remedies and redress for environmental harm and the threat of such harm.
   e Eliminate corruption in all public and private institutions.
   f Strengthen local communities, enabling them to care for their environments, and assign environmental responsibilities to the levels of government where they can be carried out most effectively.

**14** *Integrate into formal education and life-long learning the knowledge, values, and skills needed for a sustainable way of life.*
   a Provide all, especially children and youth, with educational opportunities that empower them to contribute actively to sustainable development.
   b Promote the contribution of the arts and humanities as well as the sciences in sustainability education.
   c Enhance the role of the mass media in raising awareness of ecological and social challenges.
   d Recognize the importance of moral and spiritual education for sustainable living.

**15** *Treat all living beings with respect and consideration.*
   a Prevent cruelty to animals kept in human societies and protect them from suffering.
   b Protect wild animals from methods of hunting, trapping, and fishing that cause extreme, prolonged, or avoidable suffering.
   c Avoid or eliminate to the full extent possible the taking or destruction of non-targeted species.

**16** *Promote a culture of tolerance, nonviolence, and peace.*
   a Encourage and support mutual understanding, solidarity, and cooperation among all peoples and within and among nations.
   b Implement comprehensive strategies to prevent violent conflict and use collaborative problem solving to manage and resolve environmental conflicts and other disputes.
   c Demilitarize national security systems to the level of a non-provocative defense posture, and convert military resources to peaceful purposes, including ecological restoration.
   d Eliminate nuclear, biological, and toxic weapons and other weapons of mass destruction.
   e Ensure that the use of orbital and outer space supports environmental protection and peace.
   f Recognize that peace is the wholeness created by right relationships with oneself, other persons, other cultures, other life, Earth, and the larger whole of which all are a part.

## THE WAY FORWARD

As never before in history, common destiny beckons us to seek a new beginning. Such renewal is the promise of these Earth Charter principles. To fulfill this promise, we must commit ourselves to adopt and promote the values and objectives of the Charter.

This requires a change of mind and heart. It requires a new sense of global interdependence and universal responsibility. We must imaginatively develop and apply the vision of a sustainable way of life locally, nationally, regionally, and globally. Our cultural diversity is a precious heritage and different cultures will find their own distinctive ways to realize the vision. We must deepen and expand the global dialogue that generated the Earth Charter, for we have much to learn from the ongoing collaborative search for truth and wisdom.

Life often involves tensions between important values. This can mean difficult choices. However, we must find ways to harmonize diversity with unity, the exercise of freedom with the common good, short-term objectives with long-term goals. Every individual, family, organization, and community has a vital role to play. The arts, sciences, religions, educational institutions, media, businesses, nongovernmental organizations, and governments are all called to offer creative leadership. The partnership of government, civil society, and business is essential for effective governance.

In order to build a sustainable global community, the nations of the world must renew their commitment to the United Nations, fulfill their obligations under existing international agreements, and support the implementation of Earth Charter principles with an international legally binding instrument on environment and development.

Let ours be a time remembered for the awakening of a new reverence for life, the firm resolve to achieve sustainability, the quickening of the struggle for justice and peace, and the joyful celebration of life.

## RESPECT AND CARE FOR THE COMMUNITY OF LIFE

*Allan Falconer*
University of Mississippi and Mississippi Space Commerce Initiative

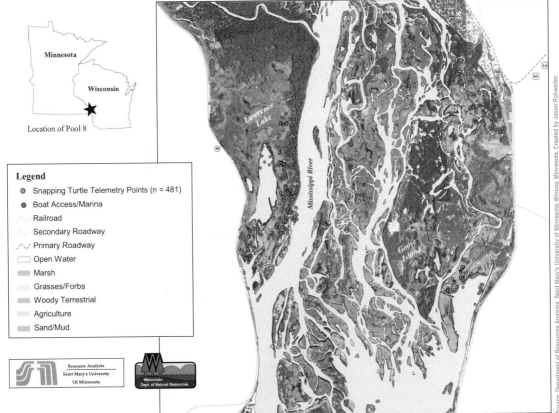

This Wisconsin Department of Natural Resources map, combining aerial photography and collected telemetry points, shows the distribution of Common Snapping Turtle populations in the Upper Mississippi River.

*Definition*

The idea on which this theme is founded is simply that of redefining geography from another angle—or, more accurately, returning to an original conception. Traditionally geography has been concerned with the diversity of life across the surface of this planet. Geographers sought to describe the variability of our planet in ideas, terms, and images of geology, geomorphology, climate, soils, vegetation, and the multiplicity of life forms that occurred naturally on the earth. Such study can easily be understood as a facet of respect and care.

*Description*

Within this framework of geographical inquiry, it was possible to understand the ways and means that people had devised and employed to support the growth of their settlement, and to have a rudimentary understanding of the basis for human socioeconomic systems. If the initial descriptions were accurate, other geographers could begin to understand the relationship between the culture and the natural resources of each region. For many years the role of the geographer was to catalog the resources of all countries and to convey a sense of the lifestyle and culture. This conception was so pervasive that it was the basis of *National Geographic* magazine. With changed technology we have seen the concept of the magazine evolve into compelling TV entertainment, in the form of National Geographic travel programs. These are important events that attract large viewing audiences.

Ironically, as international travel has become easier, the public appeal and fascination with documentaries about other countries has diminished. However, the Internet is reviving the role of the geographer as a source of information about global issues. We see

this where maps and information are available from Web sites that contain vast amounts of statistical and pictorial information.

Another consequence of easy international travel is that there has been a dramatic increase in the number of people who have traveled and who have experienced other cultures. Perhaps less fortunate is the concomitant rise in the degree of standardization of services for the tourist, and a loss of the very diversity that fascinated earlier generations, and triggered the desire to travel. The essence of geography, however, is still to be found in the understanding and appreciation of the diversity of landscape and culture being visited and observed. It is therefore more important than ever—in the face of this ease of movement and loss of variety—to understand the physical, cultural, ethnic, and sociopolitical diversity of the planet.

Respect for the earth and all its creatures is the basis for caring for the community of life and for protecting Earth's beauty for future generations. This can only be done effectively in a stable society that protects both the individual members and their economic and political structures. Such protection must occur at all scales, and it is in this kind of service where GIS may prove most useful: organizing, analyzing, and displaying the vast amounts of often incongruent data that underlies our complex systems of belief and government.

*Bibliography*

Gore, Al. 1992. *Earth in the Balance: Ecology and the Human Spirit.* New York: Houghton Mifflin Company

Monmonier, Mark. 1991. *How to Lie with Maps.* Chicago: University of Chicago Press

# ECOLOGICAL INTEGRITY

*Allan Falconer*
University of Mississippi and Mississippi Space Commerce Initiative

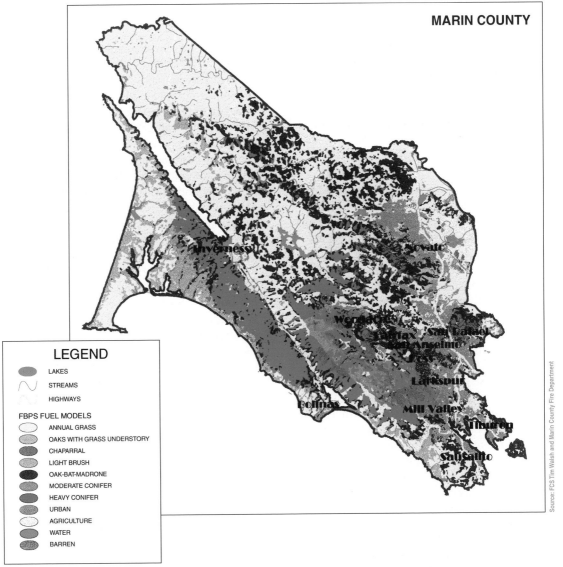

MARIN COUNTY

LEGEND

- LAKES
- STREAMS
- HIGHWAYS

FBPS FUEL MODELS

- ANNUAL GRASS
- OAKS WITH GRASS UNDERSTORY
- CHAPARRAL
- LIGHT BRUSH
- OAK-BAT-MADRONE
- MODERATE CONIFER
- HEAVY CONIFER
- URBAN
- AGRICULTURE
- WATER
- BARREN

Source: FCS Tim Walsh and Marin County Fire Department

Detailed landcover data culled from numerous organizations—United States Forest Service, California Department of Fish and Game, California Department of Forestry and Fire Protection, Humboldt State University, and others—was merged into a single map by the Marin County Fire Department. High-fuel areas, which are dominated by certain kinds of land cover and consequently more susceptible to wildfires, could be easily located, analyzed, and made safer. Special attention can be focused on suitability and sustainability of potential development.

*Definition*

The study of ecology is a recent fashion and in many ways is a simplified version of geography. In certain cases, the study of ecology is the study of natural systems and geographic locations without considering the impact of people. In this context it is a subset of classical geography, but ecology, with its emphasis on the understanding of intricate inter-relationships and mutual benefit to seemingly disparate and unconnected species and systems of life, is central to the issues of sustainable development.

*Description*

If we approach the complicated problems of human settlement as a branch of ecology, the possibility of the integrity of human interaction and natural ecosystems begins to emerge: sustainable agriculture, sustainable forestry, sustainable marine fisheries. In each and every case, the ability of the natural systems to regenerate after continuous harvesting by humans is an important ingredient in defining sustainable use. Ecology provides us with a broader context of environmental conditions as well as the limits these conditions impose on attempts at sustainability.

Maintaining soil fertility, water quality, air quality, and vegetation health are only aspects of the complex conditions that contribute to healthy animal populations. The ecological imperative to maintain the integrity of the whole is the challenge implicit in sustainability. Consider, for example, the provision of water to urban communities. This is a complex activity and includes many individual steps ranging from watershed management issues to delivery to the consumer through municipal water systems. The provision of wastewater disposal systems is an equally important task. Power companies in many cities around the world parallel the water utilities in their use of GIS in a similar way to plan and manage electrical utilities.

The Earth Charter mandates in support of ecological integrity speak of the protection and restoration of biodiversity; the prevention of harm as the best method of protection; patterns of production and consumption that safeguard natural regenerative capacities; and the advancement of the study of ecological sustainability. These smaller ideas that make up the big idea of ecological integrity may be most quickly and accurately understood if we see the civilized human world and the natural world as competing networks that need not be in conflict. Our systems (of communication, travel, transfer of power) and infrastructure must necessarily go wherever we go. Right now these networks simply overlay natural systems and the networks of nonhuman life. In many cases they interfere with, or have seriously impaired—even destroyed—the viability of these networks. Ecological integrity posits not only compatibility of systems, but a super-system, a system of systems that has each set of functions—and each subset of functions, right down to the functions of individual lives—cooperating, giving in some kind of appropriate proportion to, or in recompense of, what it takes.

The multiple aspects of cumulative effects of management decisions on the earth's biological resources can be captured in certain applications of GIS technology. Slowly we are beginning to understand the components that we must protect in order to maintain healthy ecosystems. Slowly we are beginning to understand how we may help nature help us.

*Bibliography*

Brown, Lester R., Michael Renner, and Christopher Flavin. 1997. *Vital Signs 1997: The Environmental Trends that are Shaping Our Future.* Washington, D.C.: W.W.Norton & Company, Inc.

Clarke, Robin, ed. 1986. *The Handbook of Ecological Monitoring.* Oxford: Clarendon Press.

Davidson, Donald A. 1992. *The Evaluation of Land Resources.* Harlow, UK: Longman Group UK, Ltd.

Maidment, David, and Dean Djokic. 2000. *Hydrologic and Hydraulic Modeling Support with Geographic Information Systems.* Redlands, CA: ESRI Press.

## SOCIAL AND ECONOMIC JUSTICE

*Allan Falconer*
University of Mississippi and Mississippi Space Commerce Initiative

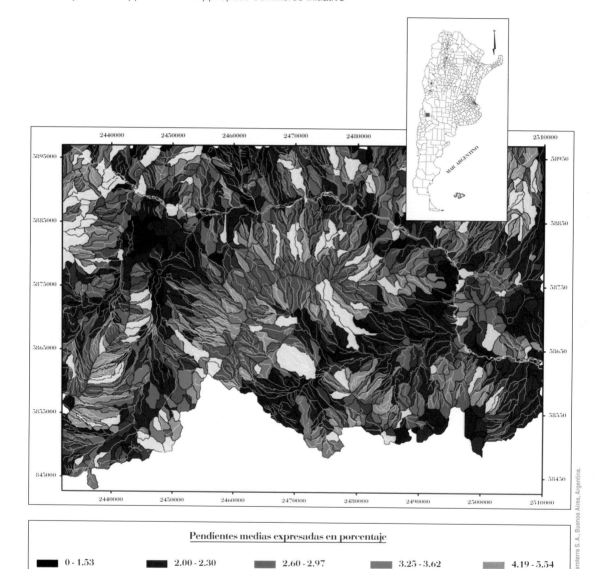

**Pendientes medias expresadas en porcentaje**

| | | | | |
|---|---|---|---|---|
| 0 - 1.53 | 2.00 - 2.30 | 2.60 - 2.97 | 3.25 - 3.62 | 4.19 - 5.54 |
| 1.54 - 1.99 | 2.31 - 2.59 | 2.98 - 3.24 | 3.63 - 4.18 | 5.55 - 10.81 |

Source: Aeroterra S. A., Buenos Aires, Argentina.

This digital elevation model (DEM) delineates basin boundaries and stream courses in a region of west-central Argentina. The average slope of each basin is expressed as a percentage and color coded. Careful consideration of the geographic features of a particular area is an important part of the process that begins with human wants and needs—in this case, oil extraction—and ends in attempts at social and economic justice.

*Definition*

Social and economic justice is a two-fold concept that has much in common with sustainable development: all derive from a fundamental sense of equity. The keeping of chickens in order to enjoy a supply of fresh eggs is an example of sustainable activity. As long as the chickens are fed and environmental needs are met the chickens will thrive and eggs will be produced. However, if we wish to eat barbecued chicken the viewpoint of the chicken will change. In a broader context, the production of chickens for meat may be considered sustainable but the individual chicken would probably prefer to be an egg producer.

*Description*

The issue of choice thus enters into this equation, alongside the concept of equity. In human societies there is an approach that suggests that a certain level of behavior is expected and that certain values can be legislated. The Constitution of the United States of America refers to certain "unalienable rights" including liberty and the pursuit of happiness. The problem is supporting this concept of rights on a global scale. If we consider our planet it is clearly impossible for each of the planet's six billion humans to share equally in each of the specific resources that exist. Although one six billionth of the world's ocean water is a measurable amount, each of us wrestling with the problem of storing, managing, and protecting our individual share of the world's oceans is impractical. Similarly, the concept of equal shares of the earth's atmosphere is elusive if it has to be reduced to a practical system.

How then are we to understand social and economic justice? Equality does not offer a rational basis, as it is a practical impossibility to allocate an equal portion of the earth to each human. Even if this were possible we would find that there were differences in the life support capability of the individual portions. Some would have sand desert, others would have ice fields, and yet others would have forest, or grasslands, or precious metals. Inevitably equal shares in the land area of our planet would produce great inequities in the economic status of members of the human race. Typically the "value" of any share would depend upon its location and therefore its geography.

Social and economic justice is addressed by the Earth Charter in four principles, each with a series of individual goals that reflect values. Over the span of human history our perceptions of the human condition have changed dramatically. What we now consider essential for a productive and fulfilling life greatly exceeds the requirements of our ancestors. The right to potable water is a reflection of our current technology and the widespread use of water to flush waste through disposal systems. The invention of the water closet in the nineteenth century has created an explosive growth in our demand for water. In the early civilizations, water was a resource that was freely available and, in a global sense, was available in abundance.

The first concern of the Earth Charter in the area of social and economic justice is to eradicate poverty. This includes the right for all humans to a basic minimum of the earth's natural resources. The basic minimum involves water that is fit to drink, air that is fit to breathe, food that is fit to eat, dwellings that are fit to live in, and safe sanitation.

These are essentially the physical elements of a sustainable and healthy environment for humans. The rights to an education, and the resources to secure a sustainable livelihood or provide a safety net for those unable to provide for themselves are all issues that can be more effectively addressed with a suitable GIS. Planning the physical resources for an education system is a demanding task. The selection of a suitable location for a school and the need for access, the population profiles of the local area to determine the size of the school, and its student profile are all amenable to GIS-based studies.

The distribution of wealth in a society can be analyzed geographically by mapping census data and revealing income by location, age, gender, education status, place of work, or size of dwelling. Unfortunately the description of the attributes does not solve the problem of equity. However it does permit an informed study and discussion of the situation because the GIS data can be verified on the ground. Simply, if the GIS is correct, a visit to any particular location will either confirm the information mapped for that place or it will not. This important test— *is it really there?*—can be carried out by anyone visiting the location defined in a GIS.

We can therefore visit areas like the refugee camps in Somalia, or the Sudan, or Palestine, or wherever the study takes us. We can use data to compile an understanding of the problems of our planet, but with the GIS technology supported by GPS systems we can visit the precise spot and see for ourselves. We can include photographs of conditions at that spot, we can insert sound tracks of interviews with the local people, and we can include the local background noise. If we care to do so, we can encapsulate the conditions that define poverty in a geographically precise way.

If our aim is to truly reveal the level of social and economic justice for each and every place on Earth, the GIS system makes this possible. We can determine if there is prejudice, if there is respect for human life, and if there is protection for human life and for the human spirit. The use of local photographs will record the effort being made to protect areas of outstanding natural beauty or of spiritual significance. Overall the information can be managed, stored, and analyzed. The value system of the society will be revealed by the impact of those decisions. That system is the core of any society's social and economic justice.

*Bibliography*

DeMallie, Raymond J., and Douglas R. Parks. 1987. *Sioux Indian Religion*. Norman: University of Oklahoma Press.

French, Hilary F. 1993. *Costly Tradeoffs: Reconciling Trade and the Environment*. Washington, D.C.: Worldwatch Institute.

Postel, Sandra. 1996. *Dividing the Waters: Food Security, Ecosystem Health and the New Politics of Scarcity*. Washington, D.C.: Worldwatch Institute.

Young, John E., and Aaron Sachs. 1994. *The Next Efficiency Revolution: Creating a Sustainable Materials Economy*. Washington, D.C.: Worldwatch Institute.

# DEMOCRACY, NONVIOLENCE, AND PEACE

*Allan Falconer*
University of Mississippi and Mississippi Space Commerce Initiative

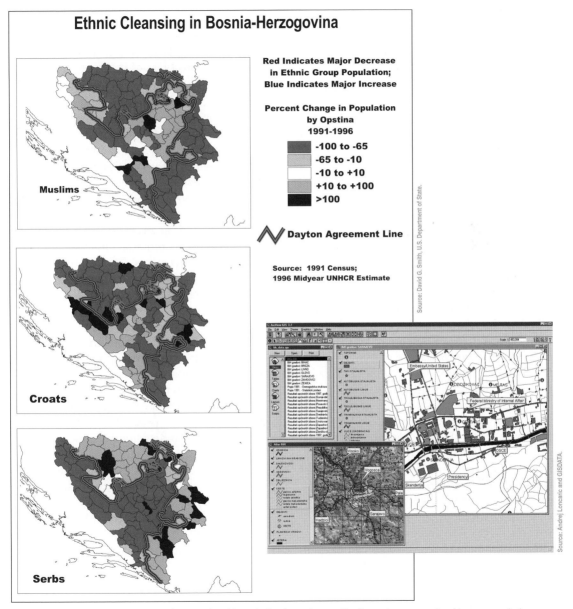

The civil wars in Yugoslavia were characterized by ethnic cleansing, or the forced movements of large populations from homelands to prison and refugee camps. These maps chart those displacements, by showing percentage changes in the population in each province of Bosnia–Herzogovina over a period of five years, from 1991–1996. The inset screen shot shows transportation infrastructure and was used in the post-war rebuilding process.

*Definition*

Sustainability depends on stability. Stability depends on peace, peace depends on nonviolent means of governance and commerce, which in turn, finally, depend on transparency and accountability. The form of government historically most amenable to such needs, and the most inclusive, is basic democracy, which can only function when citizens are educated, well-informed, and provided with access to the places and means of decision making.

*Description*

The most significant contribution that GIS can make to the cause of democracy, nonviolence, and peace is to make all these issues visible to the public. In democratic systems, the patterns of voting, the profiles of the electoral districts, and the location and the security of polling stations can all be mapped. Government facilities can be located and their accessibility to the public at large can be assessed. The spatial impact of governmental decisions can be made apparent—decisions and consequences which are or may be of particular importance to the community planning process.

GIS permits the rapid creation of maps of alternative plans so that the public can view the range of possible solutions for a planning activity. It may be the location of a new road, a new subdivision, new industry, or the positioning of a flower bed or avenue of trees in a public space. Citizens will not only be able to view the possibilities but, more importantly, vote on alternatives and even participate in interactive design processes. This can happen in development planning at any level from the decision about the placing of a new village well to an agreement about the necessity and creation of a landfill site.

Inclusive and participatory technologies like GIS expand the working definition of democracy. It is not necessarily the way for all decisions to be made in even a radically democratic society, but it does make government more responsive to the people. Some places are already using the techniques and strategies of e-commerce to make public services accessible online. To add dynamic, interactive maps to the system that, for instance, allow land parcels to be viewed so that each property owner can submit changes or improvements for taxation purposes, is now an easy step that brings GIS into the every day activity of the citizen-voter.

Online government budgets, declared land ownership, and the record of land transactions certainly would help minimize corruption in governments. "Transparent filing cabinets" would make the practice of clandestine transaction more difficult, and the violent reaction to them less common. Education in these technologies and the understanding of the data would greatly assist in the building of an enlightened electorate. In these ways GIS has a great potential to strengthen democracies and to assist in building open societies that would, by logical extension, be more conducive to peace.

Peacekeeping is an activity that has been strongly supported by GIS and associated geospatial technologies. The immediately obvious use of GIS to locate the destination for an emergency vehicle does save time and lives, and the secure tenure of property depends upon an efficient police force operating within the justice system.

At other levels these concepts apply to military activity. The deployment of armies to defend property or rights that have been infringed is a constant feature of an active military system supporting a democratic government. Border disputes are invariably based on maps of boundaries, a theme that is readily supported by GIS. Disputes on land or water may be readily resolved by use of GIS and GPS technology.

The precision and versatility of a GIS offers many benefits in the recording of political boundaries and the definition of the resources within a defined territory. The catchphrase "trust but verify" can be implemented in many ways with a GIS system that can provide accurate boundaries, and the associated resources. These resources may be mineral rights or leases, timber stands or industrial properties. Typically, the peaceful exercise of the rights of ownership requires the existence of a judicial system that is backed by an effective police force and ultimately an army. Each and every aspect of this has major geographical components. The geography of legal jurisdictions and the particular laws within each is a common concept that we all live with.

It is perhaps surprising to note that GIS and the associated technologies can so effectively extend the reach of both the governed and the governing—both sides of a democratic state. It is only if the information is kept from the citizens that this use of technology is damaging to inalienable rights and freedom. GIS can support all aspects of the information a participatory populace requires, and most of governmental functioning is inherently geographical in the first place. The application of modern geographical tools is therefore an appropriate enterprise that facilitates the sharing of knowledge and enhances the concept of just government.

## Bibliography

Buckingham, Marcus, and Curt Coffmen. 1999. *First, Break All the Rules: What the World's Greatest Managers Do Differently*. New York: Simon & Schuster.

Rose, John Kerr. 1962. Geography in Practice in the Federal Government. In *Geography in the Twentieth Century*. London: Methuen.

Taylor, Griffith. 1962. "Geopolitics and Geopacifics." In Taylor, Griffith, eds., *Geography in the Twentieth Century*. London: Methuen.

## ENVIRONMENTAL POLLUTION

*Munyaradzi Chenje*
United Nations Environment Programme

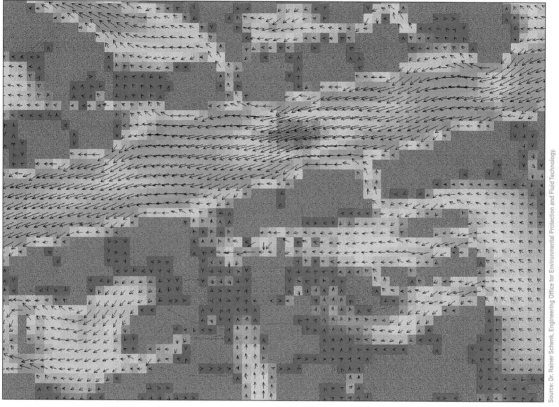

Source: Dr. Rainer Schenk, Engineering Office for Environmental Protection and Fluid Technology.

This is a three-dimensional wind-field model showing the spread of pollutants in an area of heavy traffic. Major roads and side streets act almost like rivers and tributary streams.

*Definition*

Pollution is the buildup and concentration of toxic levels of chemicals in the air, water, and land, which reduces the ability of the affected area to support life. Pollutants may be gaseous—ozone and carbon monoxide, for example; liquid—discharge from industrial plants and sewage systems; or solid—landfills and junkyards.

*Description*

Some pollutants will cause your eyes to water or your skin to break out in a rash, but most pollutants cannot be easily seen, smelled, or tasted. Their presence is nevertheless being detected in increasingly harmful quantities at the global, regional, subregional, national, local, and community levels, affecting human health as well as plant and animal life. Species extinction, reproductive mutation, human respiratory diseases, and various kinds of cancer have all been traced to the increasing toxicity of our environment.

Stratospheric ozone depletion—caused by chemicals used in the home as well as industrially—is a major threat to the welfare of the entire planet. The ozone layer protects us from ultraviolet radiation, which is responsible for sunburn, snow blindness, eye damage, skin cancer, and the premature aging and wrinkling of skin. The adoption and ratification of the 1987 Montreal Protocol to the Vienna Convention on Substances That Deplete the Ozone Layer has facilitated the phase-out of ozone depleting substances such as chlorofluorocarbons—used typically as aerosol propellants and as a coolant in refrigeration systems—and their replacement by less harmful chemicals and techniques.

On the regional and local levels, four related developments have significantly worsened air quality: growing cities, increasing traffic, rapid economic development, and higher levels of energy consumption. The course of the last two or three centuries suggests that there is a link between population and economic growth, but theories about the nature and strength of that connection remain the subject of debate: *does a rapidly growing population stimulate economic growth, or is it the other way around? Does a too-large population form a kind of natural barrier or check to otherwise unlimited economic growth? Should economies be allowed or encouraged to grow without regard to population? Is there an optimal population size for a country, a region, the planet? Does sustainability imply zero population growth and steady state economies, or are growth and sustainable communities more or less compatible?*

Whatever the answers to these questions may be, it is clear that increased levels of pollution accompany human growth. One key to managing this equation is "life cycle control" of all products, from automobiles and computers to paper and soft drinks. This is not simply recycling on both the micro (home) and macro (industrial) levels. This is recycling taken to the next step—finding ways to make the waste material of one product the fuel for another. Economic activity becomes a closed system rather than one that depends on the use of nonrenewable resources.

*Bibliography*

United Nations. 1992. *Agenda 21: The Rio Declaration on Environment and Development*. New York: United Nations.

United Nations Environment Programme. 1999. *Global Environment Outlook 2000*. Nairobi: UNEP.

*Web sites*

www.unep.net
Information, links, and references about the global environment.

www.wri.org
World Resources Institute. Earth Trends: The environmental information portal.

www.un.org/esa/sustdev/agenda21.htm
Agenda 21: The Rio Declaration on Environment and Development.

*Further reading*

Seinfeld, John H., and Spyros Pandis (contributor). 1997. *Atmospheric Chemistry and Physics: Air Pollution to Climate Change*. New York: John Wiley and Sons.

Kosobud, Richard I., Douglas L. Schreder, and Holly M. Bigep, eds. 2000. *Emissions Trading: Environmental Policy's New Approach*. New York: John Wiley & Sons.

Schnol, Jerald L. 1996. *Environment Modeling: Fate & Transport of Pollutants in Water, Air, and Soil*. London: John Wiley & Sons.

# BIODIVERSITY

*Jinhua Zhang*
United Nations Environment Programme

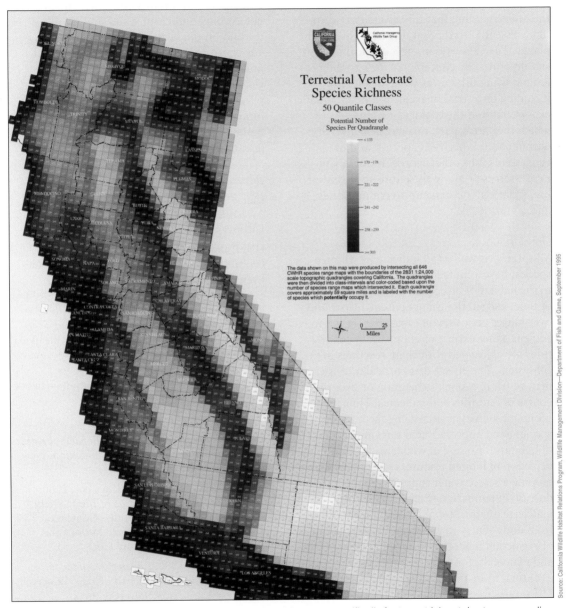

**Terrestrial Vertebrate
Species Richness**

50 Quantile Classes

Potential Number of
Species Per Quadrangle

< 133

170 –178

321 –222

241 –242

258 –259

≥ 303

The data shown on this map were produced by intersecting all 646
CWHR species range maps with the boundaries of the 2631 1:24,000
scale topographic quadrangles covering California. The quadrangles
were then divided into class-intervals and color-coded based upon the
number of species range maps which intersected it. Each quadrangle
covers approximately 59 square miles and is labeled with the number
of species which **potentially** occupy it.

0        25
Miles

Source: California Wildlife Habitat Relations Program, Wildlife Management Division—Department of Fish and Game, September 1995

This map of California deals with the potential for species richness—specifically for terrestrial vertebrates—according
to climate and ecosystem. Greatest richness is to be found along the coast and at mid-elevations, where temperatures are mild and the air is moist.

## Definition

The term biodiversity refers to the extraordinary variety of the world's organisms, the complex patterns of their interdependence, and the understanding that this diversity is absolutely essential to the viability of all life on the planet. The Convention on Biological Diversity describes the concept as "the variability among living organisms from all sources, including terrestrial, marine, and other aquatic ecosystems and the ecological complexes of which they are a part; this includes diversity within species, between species, and of ecosystems." In other words, biodiversity expresses itself along the entire spectrum of life, from genetic makeup to communities and civilizations.

## Description

All species, as well as all individuals within a species, have a finite life span. Radical changes to the habitat of a species over short periods of time, and subtler changes occurring steadily over longer periods, will cause that species to become either extinct or exotic. Both conditions are associated with chain reactions in the ecosystem. The effects of a particular cause may be felt in a single generation or over the course of centuries and millennia. Human economic activity is decreasing the number of species at an unprecedented rate: destruction of habitats (draining of wetlands, for example), depletion of limited resources (too many people tapping a scarce water supply), and the introduction of nonnative or alien species (insects inadvertently transported in a shipment of fruit from one country to another). Worse, the rate of extinction is accelerating: 38 species of birds and mammals, for example, were recorded as extinct from 1600 to 1810, compared to 112 species from 1810 to 1992.

Ironically, the breadth and depth of species diversity is essential to the human society endangering it. Food, fiber for clothing, materials for shelter and fuel, medicines, watershed protection, soil fertility, balanced composition of atmospheric elements, nutrient cycling, and clean water and air all depend on the health, abundance, and variety of species. Our aesthetic, spiritual, and recreational needs also depend on richness of diversity. In short, the physical, psychological, and emotional well-being of human beings is tied inextricably to the well-being of the other seven to twenty million (estimated) species now living on Earth.

## Bibliography

United Nations Environment Programme. 1999. *Global Environment Outlook 2000*. London: Earthscan Publications, Ltd.

UNEP and Peace Child International. 1999. *Pachamama: Our Earth, Our Future*. London: Evans Brothers, Ltd.

### Web sites

*www.unep.net*
Information, links, and references about the global environment.

*www.sustdev.org*
Inter-American Biodiversity Information Network.

## Further reading

French, Hilary. 2000. *Vanishing Borders: Protecting the Planet in the Age of Globalization*. New York: Worldwatch Institute.

Stein, B., L. Kutner, and J. Adams, eds. 2000. *Precious Heritage: The Status of Biodiversity in the United States*. The Nature Conservancy and Association for Biodiversity Information. New York: Oxford University Press.

Eldredge, Niles. 1998. *Life in the Balance: Humanity and the Biodiversity Crisis*. Princeton, New Jersey: Princeton University Press.

# CLIMATE CHANGE

*Volodymyr Demkine*
United Nations Environment Programme

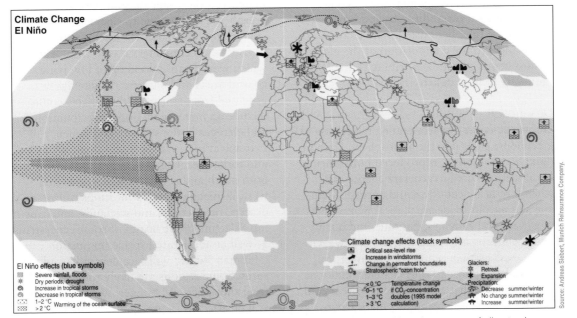

**Climate Change
El Niño**

El Niño effects (blue symbols)
- Severe rainfall, floods
- Dry periods, drought
- Increase in tropical storms
- Decrease in tropical storms
- 1–2 °C
- >2 °C Warming of the ocean surface

Climate change effects (black symbols)
- Critical sea-level rise
- Increase in windstorms
- Change in permafrost boundaries
- O₃ Stratospheric "ozon hole"

- < 0 °C  Temperature change
- 0–1 °C  if CO₂-concentration
- 1–3 °C  doubles (1995 model
- > 3 °C  calculation)

Glaciers:
- Retreat
- Expansion

Precipitation:
- Decrease summer/winter
- No change summer/winter
- Increase summer/winter

Source: Andreas Siebert, Munich Reinsurance Company.

The daily weather or meteorological map that we are all familiar with is transformed here into a map of climate change, showing areas where weather patterns have been altered above and beyond normal daily fluctuations. The data illustrated here is the result of a decade's worth of research into the effects of El Niño ocean warming.

*Definition*

Climate change is an alteration of long-standing weather patterns—as opposed to daily fluctuations—above and beyond natural climate variability observed over comparable time periods; climate changes are changes in the composition of the global atmosphere that can be attributed directly or indirectly to human activity.

*Description*

Human activities are accelerating the release of greenhouse gases into the atmosphere. Carbon dioxide, for instance, is produced both when fossil fuels are used to generate energy and when forests are cut down and burned. Methane and nitrous oxide are natural by-products of agricultural activities, but rates and quantities of emission are rising sharply as new technologies, denser concentrations of livestock, and single-crop mega-farms change conditions and techniques that are thousands of years old. Industrial processes are adding halocarbons (CFCs, HFCs, PFCs) and other long-lived gases such as sulphur hexafluoride ($SF_6$) to the mix.

By absorbing infrared radiation, these gases control the way natural energy from the sun flows through the atmosphere and is distributed by the chemical processes of weather. World climate has already begun to change as the planet adjusts itself to this new thicker blanket of greenhouse gases and attempts to maintain the balance between energy arriving from the sun and energy escaping back into space. Observations show that global temperatures have risen by about 0.6° C during the last one hundred years, with most of that change happening in the last fifty years.

Climate models predict that the global temperature will rise by about 1.4°–5.8° C by the year 2100. This change would be much larger than any climate change experienced over at least the last ten thousand years.

Such a radical change is likely to have a significant impact on the global environment. In general, the faster the climate changes, the greater the risk will be to sustainable living conditions. The mean sea level is expected to rise 9–88 centimeters by the year 2100, which would cause flooding of low-lying coastal areas and increase the damage potential from storms. Other effects could include an increase in global precipitation and changes in the severity or frequency of extreme events, such as hurricanes, droughts, and tornadoes. Climatic zones could shift both north and south, as well as east and west, displacing current locations of forests, deserts, rangelands, and wetlands, and causing a decline in the health of some ecosystems, as well as accelerated species extinction.

Human society will face new risks and pressures. Some regions are likely to experience food shortages and hunger. Water resources will be affected as precipitation and evaporation patterns change around the world. Towns and roads will be damaged, particularly by sea-level rise and increasingly severe storms. The consequences to the physical and economic health and welfare of humankind could be catastrophic.

All attempts to improve the situation will require dramatic changes in the way we use energy, as well as in our general understanding of ecological systems.

The international community is tackling this challenge through the United Nations Framework Convention on Climate Change. Adopted in 1992 and with more than 185 member nations, the Convention seeks to stabilize atmospheric concentrations of greenhouse gases at safe levels. It commits all countries to find ways to limit their emissions, gather relevant information, develop strategies for adapting to climate change, and cooperate with each other. It also requires developed countries to take measures aimed at returning their emissions of greenhouse gases to 1990 levels.

The Kyoto Protocol (an extension of Convention agreements, which outline ways to proceed) requires governments to take even stronger action. In 1997, the parties to the Convention agreed by consensus that developed countries should accept a legally binding commitment to reduce their collective emissions of six greenhouse gases by at least 5 percent compared to 1990 levels by the period 2008–2012. The Protocol also establishes an emission trading regime and a "clean development mechanism." As of the date of this publication, the Protocol has received the signatures of eighty-four countries (a signature indicates acceptance in principle) and forty-six ratifications (a ratification indicates willingness to be legally bound by the agreement). It will enter into force as international law when countries responsible for 55 percent of the world's carbon dioxide emissions have ratified it.

Many options for limiting emissions, however, are available to all nations in the short- and medium-term. Policymakers can encourage energy efficiency and other climate-friendly trends in both the supply and consumption of energy by providing an appropriate economic and regulatory framework, as well as by informing and educating consumers and investors. This framework should promote cost-effective actions, the best current and future technologies, and "no regrets" solutions that make economic and environmental sense irrespective of climate change. Taxes, regulatory standards, tradable emissions permits, information programs, voluntary programs, and the phase-out of counterproductive subsidies to oil and gas industries can all play a role. Changes in practices and lifestyles, from better urban transport planning to personal habits such as turning out the lights and riding a bicycle, are also critically important.

It will be necessary to balance concerns about risks and damages with concerns about economic development. The prudent response to climate change, therefore, is to adopt an international portfolio of positive and cooperative actions aimed at controlling emissions, adapting to new conditions and consequences, and encouraging scientific, technological, and socioeconomic research.

*Bibliography*

United Nation Environment Programme. 2001. *Climate Change Information Sheets.* Geneva: UNEP.

*Web sites*
*www.unfccc.int*
The Secretariat of the United Nations Framework Convention on Climate Change.

*www.ipcc.ch*
The Intergovernmental Panel on Climate Change.

*www.unitar.org*
The CC:TRAIN Programme.

*www.wmo.ch*
The World Meteorological Organization.

*iisd.ca/climatechange.htm*
The International Institute for Sustainable Development.

*www.gcrio.org*
The U.S. Global Change Research Information Office.

*Further reading*

UNEP. 2001. *Climate Change Information Sheets.* Geneva: UNEP.

UNEP. 2001. *Climate Change 2001: The Scientific Basis.* Contribution of Working Group I to the Third Assessment Report of the Intergovernmental Panel on Climate Change. New York and Cambridge: Cambridge University Press.

UNEP. 2001. *Climate Change 2001: Impacts, Adaptation, and Vulnerability.* Contribution of Working Group II to the Third Assessment Report of the Intergovernmental Panel on Climate Change. New York and Cambridge, UK: Cambridge University Press.

UNEP. 2001. *Climate Change 2001: Mitigation.* Contribution of Working Group III to the Third Assessment Report of the Intergovernmental Panel on Climate Change. New York and Cambridge: Cambridge University Press.

# DEFORESTATION

*Christian Lambrechts*
United Nations Environment Programme

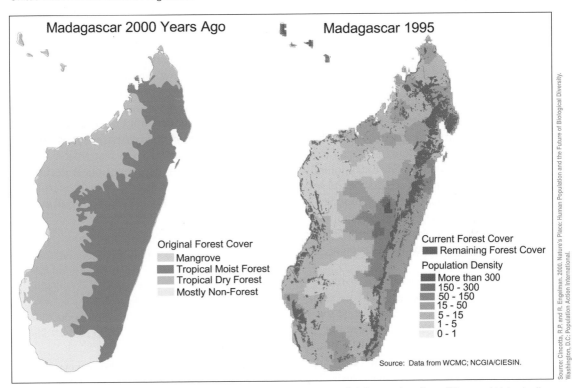

Madagascar 2000 Years Ago     Madagascar 1995

Original Forest Cover
- Mangrove
- Tropical Moist Forest
- Tropical Dry Forest
- Mostly Non-Forest

Current Forest Cover
- Remaining Forest Cover

Population Density
- More than 300
- 150 - 300
- 50 - 150
- 15 - 50
- 5 - 15
- 1 - 5
- 0 - 1

Source: Data from WCMC; NCGIA/CIESIN.

Source: Cincotta, R.P. and R. Engelman. 2000. Nature's Place: Human Population and the Future of Biological Diversity. Washington, D.C: Population Action International.

This map of the island of Madagascar is striking evidence of the extent of deforestation. One of the most biologically rich and unique spots on Earth (home to 5 percent of the world's species), it is in danger of becoming one of the least. All but 10 percent of the forests have been burned, replaced mainly by coffee plantations, cattle ranches, and mining operations. A booming population, mass migration to cities, and hard economic times complete the scenario of destruction.

*Definition*

Deforestation is the removal of tree cover for the sake of agriculture, mining operations, water impoundments, infrastructure creation and maintenance, expansion of cities, and other consequences of a rapidly growing human population.

*Description*

The world's forests have shrunk significantly over the last several thousand years. The extent of deforestation that can be directly traced and attributed to human activity has not been precisely determined. Extrapolations based on current knowledge of the soil, elevation, and climatic conditions required by forests suggest that the planet's original forest cover may have been reduced, from the time of the earliest civilizations to the present, by nearly fifty percent.

More importantly, the rate of deforestation appears to be accelerating. More than 12.5 million hectares of natural forest (an area slightly larger than Iceland) are lost every year. This loss is unevenly distributed as well. In the tropics, where the vast majority of the world's known species lives—making tropical forests both the engine and refuge of biodiversity—14.2 million hectares of natural forest are lost yearly, while in the industrialized temperate and boreal countries, natural forest cover is increasing by 1.7 million hectares per year.

Deforestation appears to be the consequence of a lack of understanding of the role forests play in human lives and the benefits they provide. As habitats decline and larger numbers of plant and animal species disappear, vital environmental services—regulation of river water flow, water filtration, soil conservation, absorption of greenhouse gases, for example—are lost as well. In the long run, deforestation undermines the foundations of the very economies, industries, and commercial interests that are most responsible for and dependent on deforestation. A decline in human well-being, in other words, is ironically the cost of unchecked development.

*Bibliography*

United Nations Development Programme. 2000. *World Resources 2000–2001: People and Ecosystems: The Fraying Web of Life.* Washington, D.C.: The World Resources Institute.

Food and Agriculture Organization of the United Nations. 2001. *State of the World's Forest 2001.* Rome: FAO Publications.

United Nations Environment Programme. 2001. *An Assessment of the Status of the World's Remaining Closed Forests.* Nairobi: UNEP.

*Web sites*
*www.ulb.ac.be/ceese/meta/sustvl.html*
A comprehensive list of Internet sites dealing with sustainable development, including organizations, projects, and activities; electronic journals; libraries; references and documents; databases; directories; and metabases.

*www.forests.org*
Forest conservation portal, vast collection of rainforest, forest, and biodiversity conservation news and information.

*www.forestinformation.com*
Offers educational content on sustainable forest management from Canadian, United States, and United Nations forestry resources. Operated by forestry companies and industry associations. Includes a kids' and teacher's section.

*Further reading*

Chew, Sing C. 2001. *World Ecological Degradation: Accumulation, Urbanization, and Deforestation 300 B.C.–A.D. 2000*. Lanham, Maryland: Altamira Press.

Rudel, Thomas K. and Bruce Horowitz. 1993. *Tropical Deforestation: Small Farmers and Land Clearing in the Ecuadorian Amazon (Methods and Cases in Conservation Science)*. New York: Columbia University Press.

Vajpeyi, Dhirendrea K., ed. 2001. *Deforestation, Environment, and Sustainable Development: A Comparative Analysis*. New York: Praeger Publications.

# FOOD PRODUCTION

*Timo Maukonen*
United Nations Environment Programme

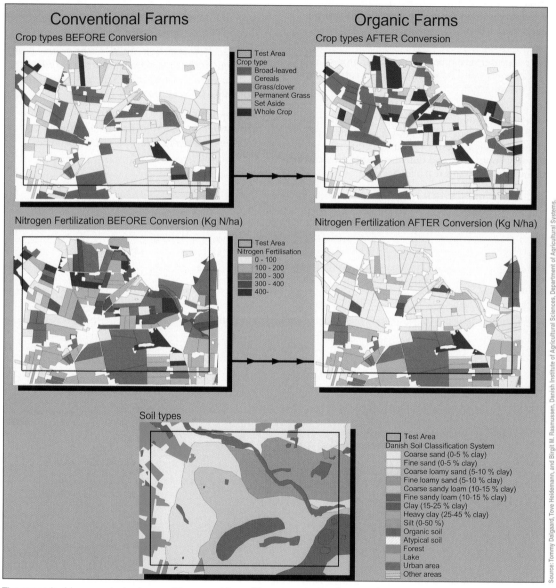

The maps in this case study show soil types and four different scenarios for use of 2,000 hectares of farmland in Denmark. The goal of the project was to reduce the amount of nitrogen (from fertilizer) leaching into the ground water of environmentally sensitive areas.

Source: Tommy Dalgaard, Tove Heidemann, and Birgit M. Rasmussen, Danish Institute of Agricultural Sciences, Department of Agricultural Systems.

*Definition*

To produce food is to cultivate, harvest, generate, or raise plants and animals that are consumed to sustain life, provide energy, and promote growth.

*Description*

The past fifty years have seen a dramatic increase in the amount of food being produced. The development of agribusiness and integrated processing and marketing systems have created new opportunities, while a general liberalization of markets has increased possibilities for export of surplus. These new strategies and technologies, however, have done more to simply increase global production than they have to reduce social disparities among producers and consumers, or to combat land degradation and ensure fertility and sustainable productivity. In short, more food is being produced, but more people are starving.

The contradiction of severe poverty and undernourishment in the midst of unparalleled plenty remains a central issue in global welfare. It is estimated that more than 820 million people in the world remain undernourished, including 790 million living in developing countries and a further 34 million living in industrialized countries and countries with economies in transition. By the year 2020, the world will have some 2.5 billion more people, and cereal demand is expected to double to two billion tons annually in the Third World.

As the arable land per capita has continued to decrease during recent decades, the increase in food production has largely been achieved by use of external inputs. However, these external inputs have come at the expense of natural control processes and resources, rendering the environment even more vulnerable. Pesticides have replaced biological, cultural, and mechanical methods for controlling pests, weeds, and diseases; inorganic fertilizers have substituted for livestock manure, composts, and nitrogen-fixing crops. The specialization of agricultural production and the associated decline of mixed farming have also contributed to the worsening situation.

While nutrients, such as nitrogen and phosphorus, are essential to agricultural production and to raising productivity, nutrients in excess of immediate crop needs can pollute surface and ground water (contamination and eutrophication), the air (acidification), and contribute to global warming (greenhouse effect). Similarly, another central farming strategy, the limiting of losses from the effects of pests, diseases, and weed competition through application of pesticides, certainly contributes to higher productivity but also poses risks to human health as well as the environment. There are international consequences to consider, too, as chemicals used in one place find their way into the food chain or one of the planet's many other systems of natural transportation, and have transboundary effects. This is particularly the case with persistent organic pollutants, or POPs.

Agriculture also plays a key role with regard to biodiversity, which is highly dependent on land use. The expansion and overspecialization of farm production and intensification of input use are considered a major cause of the sharp drop in the number of species worldwide, as well as the consequent weakening of the ecological resilience of agricultural systems.

At the same time, certain agro-ecosystems can serve to maintain biodiversity. Farming is dependent on biological services such as the provision of genes to develop improved crop varieties and livestock breeds, crop pollination, and the soil fertilization provided by microorganisms. Properly managed, these needs and services complement each other and create a perpetually renewing source of energy. Mismanagement of these services, and concomitant dependence on technological "solutions," give rise to such calamities as "mad cow disease" and less obvious problems such as cross-fertilization of genetically modified crops with wild species or landraces, and the consequent narrowing of the genetic base of crop and animal production—making farmers dependent on seed manufacturers rather than on the millennia-old method of saving seed from the harvest to use in the next season's planting.

Stress on the environment and land resources is further reinforced by natural disasters and climate-related events, such as droughts, floods, and landslides. Land degradation, soil loss, and desertification persist with particular intensity and impact for many lower-income dryland countries and less advantaged groups, endangering the livelihoods of smallholder farmers and inducing changes in land-use systems that lead inexorably to a vicious circle of further resource depletion. There is a clear cause-and-effect relationship between poverty, land degradation, and desertification; land degradation and land use; natural disasters and land use; and food contamination and production practices. The degradation of land resources is a global phenomenon but acted out at local levels. It is estimated that worldwide soil degradation affects over two billion hectares, putting at risk the livelihoods of more than one billion people.

Finally, it is not only terrestrial natural resources that continue to degrade and shrink—more than 25 percent of the two hundred main marine fisheries worldwide are overexploited, depleted, or recovering, while another 40 percent are fully exploited. Fisheries are collapsing in some parts of the world and international disputes over fish stocks are increasing. Warnings about over-fishing and the potential threat to food security among the poor are being taken increasingly seriously at the national and international levels. The research and development of aquaculture that has been undertaken in recent years, while not without environmental implications, may prove highly effective in alleviating the plundering and weakening of marine resources.

*Bibliography*

Food and Agricultural Organization of the United Nations. 2000. *The State of Food Insecurity in the World, 2000*. Rome: FAO.

International Fund for Agricultural Development. 1998. *Drylands: A Call to Action*. Rome: IFAD.

United Nations Development Programme. 2000. *World Resources 2000–2001: People and Ecosystems: The Fraying Web of Life*. Washington, D.C.: The World Resources Institute.

FAO. 2001. *Foodcrops and Shortages*. Rome: FAO.

International Food Policy Research Institute. 1999. W*orld Food Prospects: Critical Issues for the Early Twenty-first Century*. Washington, D.C.: IFPRI.

———. 1995. *A 2020 Vision for Food, Agriculture, and the Environment*. Washington, D.C.: IFPRI.

Middleton, Nick, and David Thomas, eds. 1997. *World Atlas of Desertification, 2nd Edition*. Oxford, UK: Oxford University Press and UNEP.

*Web sites*
*www.unu.edu/env/plec*
UNEP-UNU-GEF: People, land management, and environmental change.

*www.worldbank.org/poverty/data/trends/ index.htm*
World Bank, World Development Report 2000/2001.

*Further reading*

FAO. 1997. *Report of the World Food Summit*. Rome: FAO.

UNEP. 1999. *Global Environment Outlook 2000*. London: Earthscan Publications, Ltd.

IFAD. 2001. *Rural Poverty Report, 2001: The Challenge of Ending Rural Poverty*. Oxford: Oxford University Press.

Gruhn, Peter, Francesco Goletti, and Montague Yudelman. 2000. *Integrated Nutrient Management, Soil Fertility, and Sustainable Agriculture: Current Issues and Future Challenges*. 2020 Vision Discussion Paper 32. Washington, D.C.: IFPRI.

## FRESH WATER SUPPLY

*Salif Diop*
United Nations Environment Programme

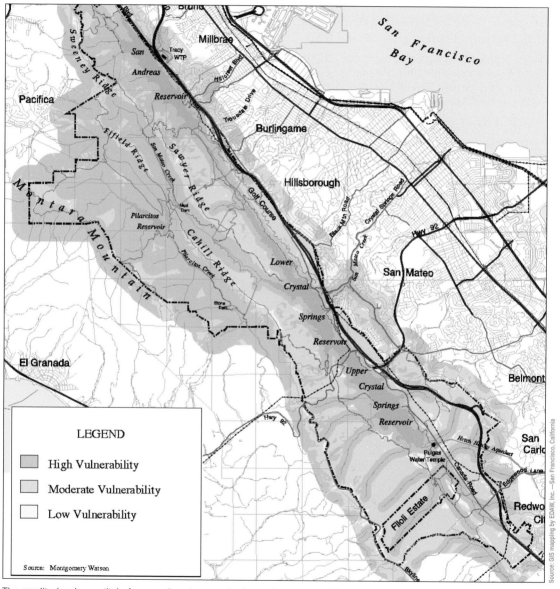

The quality (and quantity) of an area's water supply depends on several factors: soil characteristics, vegetative cover, rainfall intensity, wildlife concentration and types, and the ratio of imported water to local runoff. This map shows composite water quality vulnerability zones. The darker the green, the more vulnerable the supply is to shortage and contamination.

*Definition*

Water is a common chemical substance, with a very simple atomic structure consisting of two hydrogen atoms bonded to an oxygen atom ($H_2O$). Water is the essence of all life on the planet.

*Description*

Where water exists, life is possible. Where no water exists, no life is possible. It is nature's main solvent, capable of washing mountains to the sea and the dust from flower petals. It cleans, transports, irrigates, cools, fuels, and stabilizes the functioning of everything from a single cell to the entire planet. It is what distinguishes Earth from the rest of the known universe.

Water, in other words, is a precious commodity—our most precious commodity— but paradoxically abundant enough for its true value to be overlooked or under-appreciated—or perhaps simply misunderstood. In those areas of the world where water is scarce, issues surrounding its use are matters of life and death; some analysts suggest that the wars of the coming century will revolve around water—not oil or iron or gold or any of the traditionally valuable resources nations have fought over. Right now, one-fifth of the world's population doesn't have enough water to meet daily health and sanitation needs. Even some areas of water-wealthy nations—the western United States, for example, and northern China—where population growth has far exceeded water supply, are experiencing alarming shortages.

Explosive growth alone, however, does not account for the current water crisis. While world population tripled in the twentieth century, water use increased six times. We must look at the policies underlying the management of water resources, as well as at the ways and quantities in which water is used.

Water is made available in most developed countries via government subsidy. Because it is vital to human welfare and has been relatively abundant, it has made sense for governments to do so. But as conditions worsen, the need for conservation calls for radical shifts in regulatory policy: taxation based on use, limited expansion of irrigated agriculture, increased productivity of water (wiser use), and development of storage techniques are just a few of the emerging battlegrounds.

Some people have to walk miles to fill a bucket with water that may or may not be fresh, while others let the tap run while they brush their teeth. There is in fact enough fresh water for everybody, but fundamental problems of contamination, conservation, and equitable distribution remain very much on the center stage of global issues.

*Bibliography*

Gleick, Peter H. 2001. *The World's Water 2000–2001*. Washington, D.C.: Island Press.

World Health Organization. 2000. *Global Water Supply and Sanitation Assessment*. Geneva: WHO.

*Web sites*

*www.groundwater.com*
Ground water encyclopedia.

*www.worldwater.org*
General information on the world's water resources.

*www.adb.org/Documents/Reports/Water*
Water issues from the point of view of the Asian Development Bank.

*espejo.unesco.org.uy*
More world water information resources.

*www.aaas.org/international/atlas/contents/pages/natural03.html*
American Association for the Advancement of Science's freshwater site.

*mbgnet.mobot.org/fresh*
Missouri Botanical Garden and Evergreen Project.

*Further reading*

United Nations Commission for Sustainable Development. 1999. *Comprehensive Assessment of the Freshwater Resources of the World*. New York: United Nations.

Revenga, Carmen, et al. 2000. *Pilot Analysis of Global Ecosystems: Freshwater Systems*. Washington, D.C.: World Resources Institute.

Population Action International. 1993. *Sustaining Water: Population and the Future of Renewable Water Supplies*. Washington, D.C.: PAI.

# HEALTH AND DISEASE

*Munyaradzi Chenje*
United Nations Environment Programme

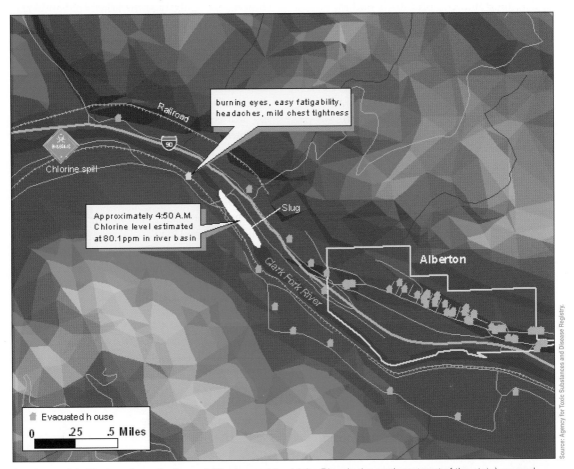

A train wreck in Montana (near the town of Alberton and the Idaho River in the northwest part of the state) caused plumes, or slugs, of lethal chlorine gas to leak from a derailed car and creep through the valley of the Clark Fork River. This map shows the location of a slug thirty-five minutes after the wreck. An atmospheric scientist specializing in plume/slug movement used a gas-dispersion algorithm to map the predicted movement and dissipation of the gas.

Source: Agency for Toxic Substances and Disease Registry.

## Definition

Health is the condition of animals, plants, and people when all the biological organs and systems that comprise their bodies are functioning normally. Another word for this condition is *homeostasis,* which means that dynamic systems (continuously operating, fluctuating, changing, and growing) are stable. Disease is the disruption of these conditions, organic interference that degrades the quality of an organism or causes death.

## Description

Environmental conditions play important roles in the health of human beings. That is to say, not only must our air and water be "healthy," but the plants and animals around us must be, too. Medical science has made astounding improvements in the technologies, techniques, and substances that promote health. People now are generally less prone to disease, and consequently live longer. However, the people of some regions of the world still must contend with grave and widespread threats to their well-being. A huge "health gap" exists between rich, developed countries and poor, undeveloped countries, where a vicious cycle of retarded development and disease makes progress next to impossible. For example, millions of people in poorer countries die each year due to environmentally related—and preventable—illnesses such as diarrhea and acute respiratory infections.

While some diseases appear to have been eliminated over the course of the last century, new ones have emerged (HIV/AIDS, for a well-known example). Malaria, a great killer from the nineteenth century, has re-emerged. It is now a health problem in more than ninety countries, with a combined total population of 2.5 billion people. Between three hundred million and five hundred million cases of malaria are reported annually, of which approximately two million prove fatal.

Disease and death in developing countries can be directly tied to poor environmental conditions, particularly at the household and local level. Many health problems are associated with poverty and lack of essential resources such as clean water and air, sanitation systems, adequate food, shelter, and fuel. Lack of drinkable water, proper sanitation, and basic hygiene is responsible for about 7 percent of all deaths and disease globally. Even developed countries are vulnerable: cases of asthma, for example, are rising dramatically in the United States. The cause? Air pollution.

## Bibliography

UNEP. 1999. *Global Environment Outlook 2000.* Nairobi, Kenya: UNEP.

World Resources Institute. 1998. *1998–99 World Resources: A Guide to the Global Environment.* Washington, D.C.; New York; and Nairobi: WRI/ UNDP/World Bank/UNEP.

## Web sites

www.unep.net
Information, links, and references about the global environment.

www.wri.org
World Resources Institute.

www.who.int/home-page
World Health Organization International.

## Further reading

Cipolla, Carlo M. 1992. *Miasmas and Disease: Public Health and the Environment in the Pre-Industrial Age.* New Haven, Conn.: Yale University Press.

Eckholm, Erik P. 1977. *The Picture of Health: Environmental Sources of Disease.* New York: W. W. Norton.

Platt, Anne E. 1996. *Infecting Ourselves: How Environmental and Social Disruptions Trigger Disease.* Worldwatch Paper 129. Washington, D.C.: Worldwatch Institute.

# URBANIZATION

*Jay Moor*
United Nations Centre for Human Settlements (Habitat)

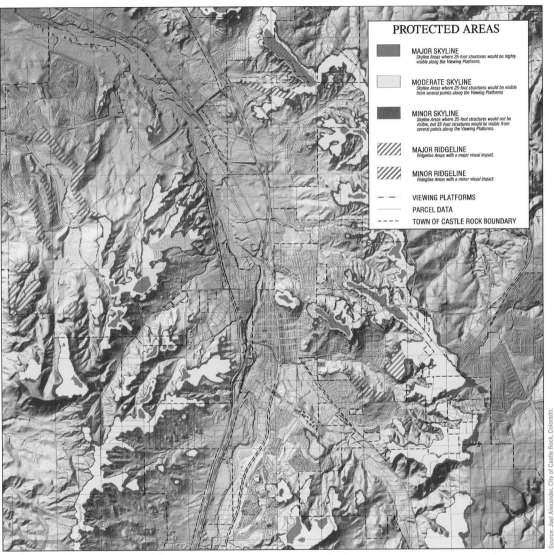

The town of Castle Rock, Colorado, is the central part of one of the fastest growing counties in the United States. In a short time, the town has had to deal with many issues related to the increased growth rate. To maintain a desirable standard of living, Castle Rock has been using GIS as an effective management tool. This map deals with visibility—what urban development can be seen from where? A digital elevation model is used to determine this information, which is used to preserve the natural appearance of skylines from key points in town.

*Definition*

Urbanization deals with the growth of the urban portion of a country's population; the diffusion of urban values and standards throughout a society; and the increase of concentrations of land covered by houses and roads.

*Description*

In 1800, less than 5 percent of the world's population lived in cities. That figure is now 50 percent of the world's six billion people and will rise to 65 percent by 2050. Urbanization is strongly associated with development and, like development, has not been evenly spread across the globe. The urban share now averages about 75 percent of total population in the most developed countries but only 25 percent in the least developed countries. As city economies expand, the promise of work and better living conditions attracts vast numbers of rural folk to urban centers. This rural-to-urban migration has been the main force behind urbanization everywhere. With the extremely rapid influx of population, however, many cities have not been able to keep up. Burdened with all the problems of growth, cities are increasingly subject to dramatic crises, especially in developing countries, which today have the highest rates of urbanization. In the cities of these countries, the main areas of concern are: not enough jobs for a growing workforce; environmental degradation; unclean water and improper waste disposal; deterioration of existing infrastructure; lack of access to land, finance, and shelter; disease; and crime. In the cities of developed countries, where rates of urbanization have slowed dramatically in recent decades, higher standards of living are, ironically, the cause of many problems.

The overuse of fossil fuels is often a direct result of wasteful urban practices and activity patterns. The extensive use of the private automobile for single purpose trips in cities, for example, unnecessarily degrades air quality and greatly increases national energy consumption that may contribute to global warming. As certain segments of their populations become more affluent, cities can become less diverse and welcoming. In some developed countries, people with means are moving to the suburbs and to gated communities, leaving the poor increasingly isolated in unhealthy and unsafe ghettos. In both developed and developing countries, cities and their economies can be made more sustainable by fostering cultural diversity, inclusive social structures, participatory systems of governance, affordable infrastructure and services, adequate shelter, conservative consumption habits, and efficient patterns of land use and transportation.

*Bibliography*

UNCHS. 1997. *The Istanbul Declaration and the Habitat Agenda*. Nairobi: United Nations Centre for Human Settlements.

———. 2001. *Cities in a Globalizing World: Global Report on Human Settlements 2001*. Nairobi: United Nations Centre for Human Settlements.

———. 2001. *The State of the World's Cities 2001*. Nairobi: United Nations Centre for Human Settlements.

*Web sites*
*www.unchs.org*
Information, links, data, reports, and references on cities and human settlements (including those in the bibliography above).

*www.citiesalliance.org*
Information, links, and projects on urban slums and slum upgrading.

*www.urban21.de*
Essays, reports, and conference proceedings on urbanization issues in the twenty-first century.

*www.who.dk/healthy-cities/hcstrat.htm*
Health plans and profiles for specific cities, how-to manual for city health planning.

*www.iclei.org*
Information, links, and local Agenda 21 projects.

*Further reading*

Drewe, Robert, ed. 1997. *The Penguin Book of the City*. London: Penguin Books.

Girardet, Herbert. 1992. *The Gaia Atlas of Cities: New Directions for Sustainable Urban Living*. London: Gaia Books, Ltd.

Hill, Dilys M. 1994. *Citizens and Cities: Urban Policy in the 1990s*. Hemel Hempstead, England: Harvester Wheatsheaf.

Jacobs, Jane. 1984. *Cities and Wealth of Nations: The Principles of Economic Life*. New York: Random House.

Mumford, Lewis. 1961. *The City in History: Its Origins, Its Transformations, and Its Prospects*. Orlando, Florida: Harcourt, Brace & Company.

Sudjic, Deyan. 1992. *The 100 Mile City*. London: Andre Deutsch.

# MOUNTAIN DEVELOPMENT

*Jinhua Zhang*
United Nations Environment Programme

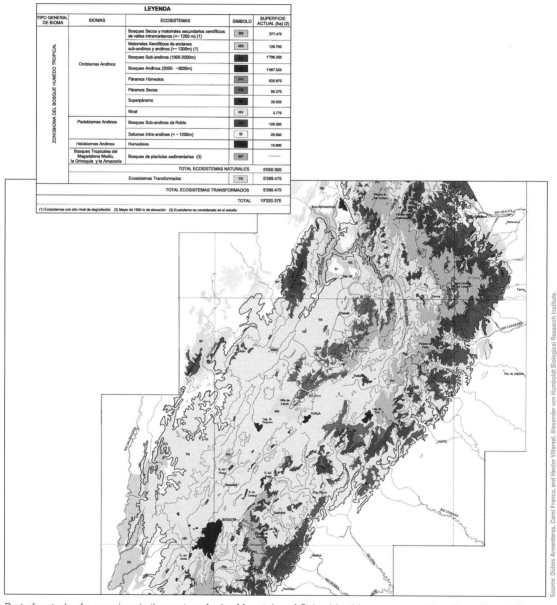

| LEYENDA | | | | |
|---|---|---|---|---|
| TIPO GENERAL DE BIOMA | BIOMAS | ECOSISTEMAS | SIMBOLO | SUPERFICIE ACTUAL (ha) (2) |
| ZONOBIOMA DEL BOSQUE HÚMEDO TROPICAL | Orobiomas Andinos | Bosques Secos y matorrales secundarios xerofíticos de valles intramontanos (<~ 1200 m) (1) | BS | 377.475 |
| | | Matorrales Xerofíticos de enclaves sub-andinos y andinos (>~ 1200m) (1) | MX | 128.700 |
| | | Bosques Sub-andinos (1000-2000m) | | 1'796.250 |
| | | Bosques Andinos (2000- ~3000m) | | 1'567.525 |
| | | Páramos Húmedos | PH | 920.875 |
| | | Páramos Secos | PS | 60.275 |
| | | Superpáramo | | 20.925 |
| | | Nival | NV | 3.775 |
| | Pedobiomas Andinos | Bosques Sub-andinos de Roble | BR | 128.350 |
| | | Sabanas Intra-andinas (< ~ 1200m) | SI | 29.950 |
| | Helobiomas Andinos | Humedales | | 16.800 |
| | Bosques Tropicales del Magadalena Medio, la Orinoquia y la Amazonia | Bosques de planicies sedimentarias (3) | BP | — |
| | | TOTAL ECOSISTEMAS NATURALES | | 5'050.900 |
| | | Ecosistemas Transformados | TR | 5'269.475 |
| | | TOTAL ECOSISTEMAS TRANSFORMADOS | | 5'269.475 |
| | | | TOTAL | 10'320.375 |

(1) Ecosistemas con alto nivel de degradación  (2) Mayor de 1000 m de elevación  (3) Ecosistema no considerado en el estudio

Source: Dolors Armenteras, Carol Franco, and Hector Villareal, Alexander von Humboldt Biological Research Institute.

Part of a study of ecoregions in the eastern Andes Mountains of Colombia, this map was put together with satellite images. The biodiversity of the region is vulnerable to development, and one of the goals of the project was to identify areas needing protection.

## Definition

Mountains are abruptly elevated land forms dominating landscapes, blocking pathways for transportation, and impeding the movement of air and water.

## Description

Mountains occupy about 20 percent of Earth's land surface, and are important sources of water, energy, and biodiversity. About 10 percent of the world's population lives in the mountainous areas, and about half of the world's population depends on the mountain resources in some way. Mountains are important factors in mining, forestry, agriculture, and tourism. Mountain ecosystems are fragile, dynamic, and complex, particularly associated with the high frequency of natural disasters such as floods, landslides, and volcanic eruptions. Global warming is causing most of the world's mountain glaciers to retreat, some of which are the major sources of water for millions of people.

The Rio summit in 1992 successfully placed these mountain issues on the political agenda (as reflected in chapter 13 of Agenda 21). However, sustainable mountain development in the twenty-first century can only be successfully undertaken by mountain people themselves, with the support of sound national economic policies and increased international cooperation.

## Bibliography

United Nations. 1992. *Agenda 21*. New York: UN.

## Web sites

www.mountains2002.org
www.unep-wcmc.org
United Nations Environment Programme–World Conservation Monitoring Centre, provides information for policy and action to conserve the living world.

www.icimod.org.sg
International Centre for Integrated Mountain Development, sustainable livelihoods for mountain communities.

# RURAL DEVELOPMENT

*Joyce Foresman*
International Center for Remote Sensing Education

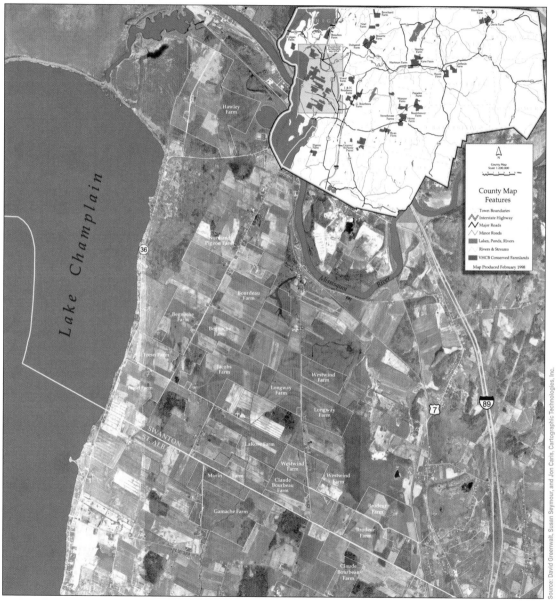

This GIS map is based on aerial photographs of Franklin County in Vermont. Land-use and land-cover data was laid over the photograph, allowing a conservation board and Vermont legislators to understand farm size and proximity, and consequently to secure funding.

*Definition*

Rural land is characterized by agriculture and farming, low population density, low concentrations of structures, nonurban lifestyles and values, and large open or undeveloped areas.

*Description*

While the population of the world's cities continues to increase sharply and spread outward, a substantial number of people continue to live in rural settlements. This is especially so in developing countries, where weak infrastructure, few services, and toxic technologies contribute significantly to the degradation of living conditions. Decreasing employment opportunities in rural areas increases as the rate of rural-to-urban migration increases, causing employment opportunities in rural areas to decrease, further complicating the problem and creating yet another of unsustainability's vicious circles.

Another grave consequence of urban expansion is the transformation of forests, wildlands, and wetlands into agricultural land and human settlements, in effect (and often literally) paving over natural filtration and cleaning systems, decreasing biodiversity, and altering the ways and means of Earth's maintenance of itself.

Urban and rural areas are interdependent economically, socially, and environmentally, making their reconciliation and mutual welfare one of the most important themes in the sustainability movement.

*Bibliography*

*The Habitat Agenda: Goals and Principles, Commitments, and Global Plan of Action.* United Nations Conference of Human Settlements (Habitat II). Istanbul, Turkey, 3–14 June 1996.

*Web sites*

www.futureharvest.org
Future Harvest commissions research, promotes partnerships, and sponsors projects that bring the results of research to rural communities, farmers, and their families in Africa, Latin America, and Asia.

www.attra.org
Introduction to permaculture—appropriate technology transfer for rural areas. Concepts and resources—alternative farming systems. Good primer and collection of links on permaculture (sustainable farming).

www.foundation.novartis.com/atoz/agriculture_links.htm
Online agricultural and rural development directories and resources from around the world.

indigo.ie/~word
W.O.R.D. Online. Wexford Organization for Rural Development.

*Further reading*

Anderson, Teresa, Alison Doig, Dai Rees, and Smail Khennas. 1999. *Rural Energy Services: A Handbook for Sustainable Energy Development. Intermediate Technology.* Sterling, Virginia: Stylus Publishing.

Flora, Cornelia, ed. 2001. *Interactions Between Agroecosystems and Rural Communities.* Boca Raton, Florida: CRC Press.

Shepard, Andrew. 1997. *Sustainable Rural Development.* New York: Palgrave Publications.

# POVERTY REDUCTION

*Joyce Foresman*
International Center for Remote Sensing Education

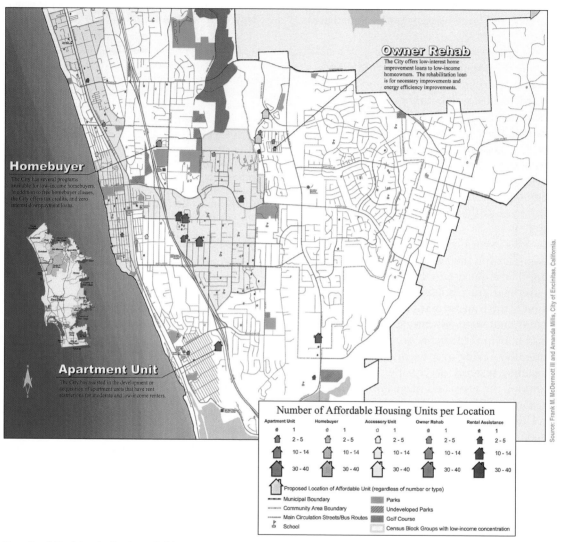

Source: Frank M. McDermott III and Amanda Mills, City of Encinitas, California.

The city of Encinitas in Southern California needed to find areas and lots suitable for development of low-income housing. Considering many factors, such as population density, proximity to services, and distribution of low-income households, the city was able to put lots of information on a single map. Working with Habitat for Humanity, they were able to build several single-family homes.

*Definition*

Poverty reduction entails the identification of people living in conditions characterized by the availability of little or no money, goods, or means of support, and the development of means to alleviate or ameliorate those conditions.

*Description*

Poverty is perhaps the greatest challenge humanity has faced. The total number of people living in poverty in urban areas has increased in recent years, even though the total percentage of people in poverty worldwide is down—not just in developing countries, but in developed countries as well. The day to day misery that poverty causes goes without question (or should); apart from that misery, poverty strikes at the very heart of the concept of sustainable development: it alienates citizens from the institutions that govern them, the decision making, planning, implementation, and management of programs that are supposed to raise the quality of their lives. Sustainability depends on the cooperative actions of individuals and the communities in which they live. Practical tools must be established to promote and sustain participatory action by local governments and communities and to communicate proper and effective political commitment. Encouraging citizens to identify their problems, facilitating their efforts to address their social and economic needs collectively, and developing community-based planning maps and models for the future pooling of resources are essential to the health and well-being of the entire world.

*Bibliography*

Ezigbalike, Chukwudozie. 2001. *Poverty Reduction*. Nairobi: SDI Workshop.

United Nations Centre for Human Settlements (Habitat). 1997. *Proceedings of the International Conference on Urban Poverty*. Florence, Italy, 9–13 November 1997.

United Nations Centre for Human Settlements (Habitat). 1998.

United Nations Centre for Human Settlements (Habitat). 2001. *From Structural Adjustment Programmes to Poverty Reduction Strategies: Towards Productive and Inclusive Cities*. International Forum on Urban Poverty (IFUP), Fourth International Conference, Marrakech, Morocco, 16–19 October 2001.

*Further reading*

Baker, Judy L., and Margaret E. Grosh. 1994. *Measuring the Effects of Geographic Targeting on Poverty Reduction: LSMS Working Paper, No. 99*. Washington, D.C.: World Bank.

McKinley, Terry. 2001. *Macroeconomic Policy, Growth and Poverty Reduction*. New York: St. Martin's Press.

Wilson, Francis, Nazneen Kanji, and Einar Braathen, eds. 2001. *Poverty Reduction: What Role for the State in Today's Globalized Economy?* (Crop International Studies in Poverty Research). London: Zed Books.

World Bank. 1992. *Poverty Reduction Handbook*. Washington, D.C.: World Bank.

# METHODS AND TOOLS

*Tim Foresman*
Executive Science Advisor for the United Nations Environmental Programme

## SPATIAL THINKING AND GEOGRAPHIC INQUIRY

The German philosopher, Immanuel Kant, declared all knowledge to be part of three fundamental forms: entities, time, and space. Space represents the fundamental glue by which we put together our ideas of entities, or things, at a particular time or period. The harnessing of space, or spatial thinking, is the essence of geographic inquiry. How humans interact with each other and their environment makes up the study of geography. Observing and studying the conditions and trends of humans and their environment, including the litany of fluxes within this human ecosystem—such as information, natural and manufactured resources, energy, and other valued commodities or capital—is what geographers do. With the advent of concern for sustainable development, the geographer's trade has become a linchpin in our attempts to understand the human ecosystem, maintain commerce, support human needs for shelter, food, clothing, and security, and preserve ecological goods and services. As the world develops the will to address these issues and the cooperative partnerships necessary to adjust human activities in ways that mitigate and regulate unsustainable practices, the application of spatial thinking and inquiry will be appropriate throughout the range of the decisions and activities involved. This

mode of thinking, whether we are conscious of it or not, involves a method, a method of geographic inquiry. Through the integration of geographic inquiry with spatial analytic and management tools, major advances in the perception and understanding of our world can be brought to the forefront of local and global actions.

Geographic inquiry is similar to the approaches, strategies, and tactics used in other disciplines and types of structured research; that is the basic scientific method. This approach enables the structured assembly of understanding about patterns of people moving through space and time, the reasons underlying those patterns, and the causes and effects in the web of life. As a scientific structure, this approach also allows for repeatability of results thereby promoting the application of those results to the legal and engineering communities that dominate the worlds of commerce and governance. Knowing where something is and how its location determines its characteristics and relationships with other phenomena is the foundation of geographic thinking. From this foundation, we can shape a perspective of the world and all that's in it. We can therefore create a common understanding of the world and its conditions, which are essential to garner our collective will in seeking sustainable solutions to the major challenges facing humankind.

Below are the steps of geographic or spatial inquiry. They represent approaches that scientists, government officials, business people, and concerned citizens might use to better manage our planet and develop behaviors that will sustain life for perpetuity. These basic steps or stages in understanding and actions are:

1  Formulate and ask spatially relevant questions.

2  Locate and acquire spatially relevant data and information resources.

3  Harness the geographic elements of data and explore their meaning.

4  Conduct geographic information analysis.

5  Generate visual products and act upon spatial reasoning and understanding.

*Formulate and ask spatially relevant questions*

In thinking about a topic or place, we first must identify the relevant factors or significant issues. Observations about these factors or issues need to be structured into the form of a question, such as *why do these particular trees show signs of stress?* or *how do the types of businesses change along a river or highway?* or *what will the impact be for the ecology of an area and its people if a forest is cleared of trees?* Turning the elements of observation into a spatially explicit question enables focused study of a problem. Geographic questions can range from simple *where are things?* to *how do things change between here and there?* to deeper questions, such as *why does this thing change between here and there?* Thus, we might be capable of formulated and therein understanding *where do songbirds nest and what are their*

*critical habitat requirements?* or *why is there drought in this region while another region is flooded?* or *what is the result of refugees moving from this land across the border to another place?* A well-formulated question allows for a structure that will illuminate the many spatial underpinnings of humankind's activities, their environmental dimensions, our responses, and the consequences of these activities.

*Locate and acquire spatially relevant data and information resources*

Once the spatial inquiry has been formulated, the process of identifying the relevant data and information resources begins. These resources for the issue at hand should encompass the three dimensions of Kantian knowledge: space, time, and subject matter (herein focused on or related to sustainable development).

WHAT IS THE GEOGRAPHIC FOCUS OF THE RESEARCH?

In studying a country in relation to others, the inquiry might require country-level data, and would need data for the country of interest as well as the neighboring countries or those affected by transboundary elements. Defining the geographic focus will allow for defining the appropriate scale (global, regional, or local) of the inquiry, and will assist in defining the full extent (a town, a country, a region, a continent, or the globe) of the inquiry.

FOR WHAT PERIOD OF TIME IS THE DATA NEEDED?

Answering questions about things happening today will require the use of the most current data and information available. However, many questions require the use of trajectory or trend analysis to determine patterns over time, and these questions become clearer and sharper if they are incorporated within a historical perspective. Temporal dimensions are critical to projecting into the future scenarios or models of what may be expected from the continued actions or inactions around a specific set of circumstances. Collecting historical data is fraught with challenges due to the requirement to define the accuracy of data, after the fact.

FOR WHAT SUBJECT AND SPECIFIC TOPIC IS THE DATA NEEDED?
It is essential to thoroughly examine the topical aspects of the data and information resources needed to formulate a study or assessment, to recommend policy, or implement action. Population information may be a central theme to a study, but transboundary migration is the actual focus. Data requirements must be carefully dissected to clearly define the information requirements for an investigation. The sharper the focus of a study, the less likely will be the wasted energy and cost for use of irrelevant or redundant data.

Often, the requisite geographic data can be readily available from national and international data repositories or research institutions, already in digital formats downloadable from the Internet. This condition is rapidly improving as the network of international and government institutions continue to create information networks with well-documented data resources. Occasionally data needs to be created, or reformatted from converted sources of data into more appropriate forms. The rise of the Internet and exponential increases in computer speeds and capacities has greatly facilitated the ability to acquire authoritative information. This explosion of data means that one can locate materials in a wide range of formats, at multiple scales, and with variable quality. After a thorough tracking of what data is readily accessible and recording the quality

of the source information, the identification of information gaps and whether there are critical components missing to answer the question is required. In the real world, missing data is almost always an element of the definition of a problem, and solutions often require acknowledging these gaps while attempting to address the initial formulated question.

*Harness the geographic elements of data and explore their meaning*
Conversion of data and information resources into maps, tables, and charts is the first step in harnessing geographic data. Maps are especially valuable, because they give a powerful view of patterns, or how things change over space. Maps also allow for integration of different kinds of data from different sources—pictures (aerial photos, satellite images) and features (roads, rivers, political and administrative boundaries)—in layer after layer. Exploration of the data can be accomplished through a variety of combinations. Examination of individual entities should include an evaluation of the spatial context of their setting. *What is near, adjacent, connected, or far away? How are spatial phenomena related to things around them: mountain and streams, cities and coastlines or rivers, agriculture and deforestation?* Creativity and keen observation are traits of a good investigation.

For any one set of data, there are many methods to aggregate, compile, and represent the information through statistics. By integrating maps with data tables, charts, and other representations, some patterns may begin to appear, patterns that might lead to redefinition of the original inquiry and thereby require additional data acquisitions. Refinement and iteration of thought is common and appropriate in this exploratory phase. For example, when first studying regional rainfall patterns, the necessity of precise locations of mountain ranges may not have been anticipated, but with orographic influences proving essential to the analysis of the problem, this data must now be included.

Using a GIS, this kind of data investigation and visual exploration is relatively straightforward. GIS technologies enable the harnessing of geographic elements that allow for the overlaying of one layer of information upon another. By changing the map symbols or representation of elements, altering the sequence of layers, or zooming in to specific regions of the map presentation, patterns and spatial relationships may become more readily discernable and amenable to discussion and follow up analysis.

*Conduct geographic information analysis*
After creatively exploring the relationships between and amongst elements of an investigation, attention should be focused on the information and maps that appear to best explain or answer the questions. Using carefully constructed queries can highlight key comparisons or expose patterns that lay hidden or seem counterintuitive during the initial explorations. GIS analysis includes focus on relationships between layers of information; making inferences about the distribution of entities or things; and calculating the degree to which the presence of something or action affects the presence or character of something else. Deeper questions begin to emerge from the analytical process—*why is it there?* and *so what?* Predictions of outcomes can then proceed; that is, the formulation of hypotheses or scenarios based on improved understanding of cause and effect and spatial relationships. For instance, discovery that patterns of traffic accidents in a community occur at certain east–west oriented intersections may promote inquiry to similar patterns in other communities.

The power of the computer becomes especially helpful in the analytic phase of sustainable development investigations. Since GIS data is made up of map representations and data tables of feature characteristics, a GIS can facilitate solving queries and identifying key entities. Asking a computer to *find all cities of one million or more people where rainfall is less than 10 inches per year with greater than 10 percent infant mortality* is a simple operation if all the information has been geocoded and linked to an investigation. While GIS is extremely quick to answer such queries, the human analysts are essential to formulate and implement the processing of automated queries. Building models of the analytical process is an important aspect of the documentation of investigative studies, in that it allows for other collaborators and reviewers to fully appreciate the methods, thought processes, and results. Reviewers will likely stimulate additional aspects of the analytical process by providing feedback of *what if* scenarios or questions.

The power of manual map overlays, using transparent sheets to portray various themes or thematic data layers over a common base map, was unveiled by Ian McHarg as the key to designing human activities in harmony with nature. These methods had proven value before the advent of computers and remain a powerful method to communicating with groups of people in small and rural settings, as well as in conference or workshop meetings.

At the final juncture of the analytical process, the focus will be on drawing conclusions from the materials that were compiled and processed into maps, map overlays, charts, and analytical modeling or scenario building. Conclusions may arise based on recognition that important information needed to answer a question does not exist. Defining knowledge that critical information is needed to solve a problem is new knowledge by itself and not a wasted exercise. The Millennium Ecosystem Study was manifest from a recognition that critical and basic information was lacking about our planet's ecological resources and services. The important aspect of our geographic method is that better understanding of a condition or issue will now exist and that more components of the sustainability puzzle will have been pieced together using spatially-oriented knowledge.

*Generate visual products and act upon our spatial reasoning and understanding*
By using a GIS to weave data together from multiple sources, transforming it in the process to comprehensible information on which to base decisions, the geographic method can lead to community action. The idea is to bring the new understanding of our planet's systems and the interactions within the human ecosystem to the appropriate community for actions supporting sustainability. Communication is key to sharing lessons learned, identifying the important characteristics from an investigation, and involving people in the actions and solutions process. Communication, enhanced through GIS-based spatial visualization, is essential to encouraging involvement, negotiating consensus, and implementing carefully planned, community supported sustainable actions. The depletion of ozone over the Antarctic is an example of how global action was initiated once a visualization of the magnitude of this anthropogenic impact was communicated.

Good governance and effective citizenship and influence over the decision making process around the planet is needed to promote coordinated and integrated understanding of the relationships between diverse forces of nature and humankind. Awareness and comprehension of the conditions and trends of the planet's systems is not sufficient to affect

sustainable systems in the future. Knowledge needs to be comprehensive and needs to be communicated and shared at all levels of comprehension. The pace of change and the challenges facing humans and the planet will not allow for missing links, overlooked facts, or excluded parties in the solution to problems which are interconnected to each other in a web of cause and effect.

This "conveyance of comprehension" may require, for example, the preparation of charts and maps of the environmental conditions around a school to display the distribution of diseased vegetation and their role in reducing energy resources for urban cooling, or for a town council regarding options for reducing agricultural pesticides due to the impact on estuarine ecosystems and the cost of protecting citizen's health downstream. Visualization of results may assist in recruiting local business allies to provide resources to communities far away, or in changing policies and legislation for regional energy management due to the environmental externalities on the other side of a nation. Understanding the widespread linkages and helping others to see how their lives are affected means "thinking globally, acting locally." My Community, Our Earth (MyCOE) is another global initiative to take this classic bumper sticker phrase into educational action and assessments for improving our chances for a sustainable future. Through the effective application of the spatial thinking and geographic inquiring, in combination with the communication of visually stimulating results, the steps toward sustainable pathways for the future of our communities are set.

# CHECKLIST OF EQUIPMENT AND DATA

## Equipment

__ Camera
__ Charts
__ Compasses
__ Computers
__ Global Positioning System (GPS)
__ Survey equipment
__ Graphs
__ Measuring tapes
__ Transparent sheets
__ Notebook to record your project and references

## Images

__ Aerial photographs
__ Satellite imagery for large areas

## Maps

__ Boundaries delineated
__ County/city road map
__ Topographic maps

## Software

__ GIS
__ Spreadsheets
__ Word processing
__ Database management

## Data

### EXISTING BIOLOGICAL DATA

__ Published inventories
__ Field notes and memory
__ Government, local, and national level published reports

### EXISTING PHYSICAL DATA

__ Geology maps
__ Maps showing hazards, floodplains, etc.
__ Topographic maps
__ Aerial photographs
__ Satellite imagery for large scale
__ Photographs

## Data analysis

__ Comparison of recent to past
__ Field notes/inventory
__ Placement of information into data banks (files)

## Display format

__ Maps, using either digital or manual methods, showing the changes
__ Reports describing your theme, approach, results, and summary
__ Photographs

# TOOLS

Geographic-oriented research does not have to rely on data that an individual collects in the field. Good investigations usually rely on a collection of "secondary" or "tertiary" data sources and information in combination with field verification sampling or assessments. A wide range of tools may be required for any study in sustainable development. These tools will come from the complete array of scientific disciplines and techniques. What glues these research methods together and makes them amenable to quantitative display is the accounting of the spatial dimension of data, and therefore the need to spatially enable or attribute field data, or other source data.

Local, community, regional, national, and global investigation may use a combination of tools listed herein, and more, as long as the focus remains on defining and communicating issues related to the spatial relationships of sustainable development in the world. The success of an investigation or project relies more on the clear definition of the issues and a good set of questions than on the specific tools applied. Spatial analysis and geographic thinking are the critical elements to which the proper tools should be applied and within which sustainability science should proceed.

*Bibliography*

Kant, Immanuel. 1999. *Critique of Pure Reason.* Paul Guyer and Allen W. Wood, eds. Cambridge, UK: Cambridge University Press.

McHarg, Ian L. 1969. *Design with Nature.* New York: John Wiley & Sons.

Foresman, T. W. 1998. *The History of Geographic Information Systems: Perspectives from the Pioneers.* Upper Saddle River, New Jersey: Prenctice Hall.

The Millennium Ecosystem Study. 1991. *www.millenniumassessment.org*

# GIS FOR BEGINNERS

## THINKING SPATIALLY

*"The most incomprehensible thing about the world
is that it is comprehensible."*

—Albert Einstein

### Floods in Kathmandu

This year's monsoon has brought more rain
than usual to the country—even in Kathmandu, where the increasing population and
the scarcity of land means that too many
homes are being built on farms and lowland,
without regard for either sustainability or
susceptibility to disaster.

Although the Bagmati and the Bishnumati
are the two major rivers flowing through
the Kathmandu valley, it is the Tukucha
and Samakhusi rivers that give trouble more
frequently—their banks have been heavily
built up with large buildings and squatter
settlements.

Seeing this story, a person who is familiar
with Kathmandu can visualize the scenario.
He knows these problem areas, how these
localities look, and the types of houses that
are prevalent in these areas. This is called
a "mental map." It is generated from information stored consciously or unconsciously
in a person's brain over the years. However,
mental maps are not sufficient if we want
to understand the problem in more detail
or devise a remedy. Planners, engineers, and
construction workers need maps and drawings to guide them. But sometimes maps
alone are not enough. Super maps, capable of
storing and displaying vast amounts of data,
have become increasingly necessary.

Figure 1: Kathmandu valley from space, with rivers overlain

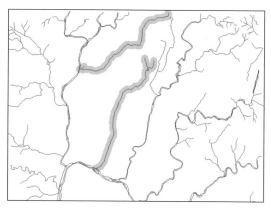

Figure 2: Area within 150 meters of Tukucha and Samakhusi Rivers

Figure 3: Wards that are intersected by the buffer zone

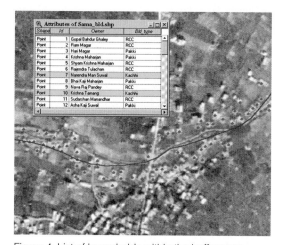

Figure 4: List of households within the buffer zone

To find the areas that are most likely to be affected by floods, let's demarcate the area within 150 meters of these rivers (figures 1 and 2). This buffer area can be considered as the flood-prone zone. Now, if we want to make plans to improve the situation, we need to involve local bodies such as the ward offices. We should identify the stakeholders; these are the wards falling in these flood-prone areas and the households that are likely to be affected by flooding. For this, we need to identify the wards and then the households that lie within the buffer zone (figures 3 and 4).

When we do so, we are engaging in spatial reasoning, the essential human factor in any GIS.

*Buying a new house*

People from all over Nepal migrate to Kathmandu valley looking for jobs (figure 5). After some time, they think of buying a piece of land and building a house. However, there are many constraints to overcome before this dream can come true.

The first task is to find suitable land. With the rapid urban expansion in the valley, it is becoming more difficult to find good places for living. People have their preferences, but there are common issues that need to be considered.

The land should be close enough to basic infrastructure such as roads, water, and electricity supplies. In Kathmandu, facilities such as water and electricity are dependent on accessibility to roads. Figure 6 shows the area within 500 meters of major roads.

We have already seen that there are places in the heart of the Kathmandu valley that are frequently affected by floods. Figure 7 shows the area at least 500 meters from major rivers.

Also, the land should be safe from natural hazards, such as landslides, that occur on steep slopes. The area that has a slope greater than ten degrees is shown in figure 8. This land would not be suitable for building purposes.

Excluding all land that is not suitable because of road, river, or slope criteria, we find the area that is suitable for building a residence (figure 9).

We have used information based on geographic features—rivers, roads, and slope—and their relationships to solve our problem.

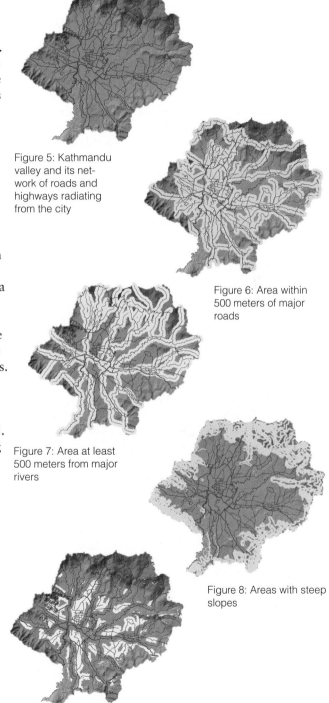

Figure 5: Kathmandu valley and its network of roads and highways radiating from the city

Figure 6: Area within 500 meters of major roads

Figure 7: Area at least 500 meters from major rivers

Figure 8: Areas with steep slopes

Figure 9: Area suitable for building

*Let's have a broader outlook*

So far, we have discussed our desire to build a house and the need for improvements in the urban environment of Kathmandu valley. However, what is the scenario if we look at the country as a whole? We know that there is a lot to be done in all sectors and regions of the country to improve the livelihoods of the people. However, with our limited resources it is not possible to meet all the needs at once. How then do we identify the most pressing needs?

Let us plot these figures on a map and see how it looks (figure 10).

Similarly, we can look at the indices for poverty and deprivation, women's empowerment, and socioeconomic and infrastructural development in Nepal on a map (figures 11, 12, and 13).

We can see that when we plot values on a map, things become clearer and it is easier to make decisions. In this example, we can see that the situation in the far western region is the poorest in all indices. Therefore, greater focus is needed on development in this region.

What we see here is that when we add a spatial or geographic component to our analysis, we have a better picture of the real-world scenario. This is often called "spatial thinking." It gives us better insight of our problems and allows us to make better decisions.

The use of computerized information systems is a growing part of our everyday life. GIS is one such system that uses the power of computers to answer questions related to location by arranging and displaying data about places in a variety of ways, such as maps, charts, and tables. In the following chapters, we will discuss more about maps, mapping, and GIS.

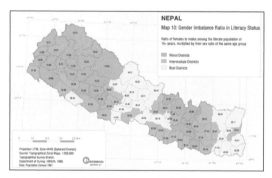

Figure 10: Gender imbalance ratio in literacy status

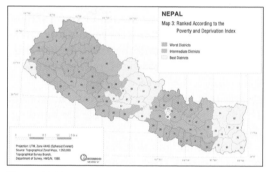

Figure 11: Poverty and deprivation index

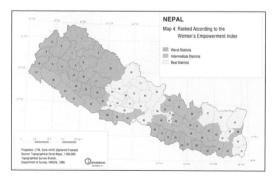

Figure 12: Women's empowerment index

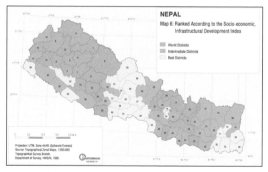

Figure 13: Socioeconomic and infrastructural development index

# YOU AND MAPS

*"A journey of a thousand miles starts in front of your feet."*

—Lao Tzu

After going through the examples in the previous section, you have probably noticed one thing—we used lots of maps to give a clear picture of the areas discussed. We have seen that maps are powerful means of conveying messages related to places or location. Now let us look at maps in more detail.

A map is a two-dimensional picture of a place, designed to give you a better understanding of that place. Maps are made for many reasons and, therefore, they vary in content and context. Different symbols are used to represent the features of the environment on a map. These features are explained in a map's legend.

## Some examples
### A PHOTOGRAPH
A photograph shows a place as our eyes see it. However, the area that is viewed on the ground is limited. It is often difficult to see a substantial landscape in one photograph.

### AERIAL PHOTOGRAPH
A photograph taken from an aircraft is known as an aerial photo (figure 14). These photographs are normally taken to prepare maps of an area. Aerial photographs give a "birds-eye" view of the earth's surface. Features on Earth look different from above; consequently, field experience is needed to make correct interpretations of these photographs.

Figure 14: Aerial photograph

SHADED RELIEF MAP

A shaded relief map shows how an area looks when sunlight is shining on it from a particular direction (figure 15). It gives an impression of the nature of the terrain. We can visualize whether an area is flat or rugged by looking at these maps.

TOPOGRAPHIC MAP

A topographic map (figure 16) shows the shape of the earth's surface by contour (elevation) lines. Contours are the imaginary lines that join points of equal elevation on the surface of land above or below a reference surface such as mean sea level. These maps include symbols that represent features such as streets, buildings, rivers, and forests. Topographic maps are used by most applications as the base map on which other features or phenomena are referenced.

ROAD/TOURIST MAP

Road maps show people the route for travelling from one place to another. They show some physical features such as rivers and forests, and political features such as cities and towns (figure 17). Normally, tourist maps emphasize the locations of monuments and tourist spots.

Figure 15: Shaded relief map

Figure 16: Topographic map

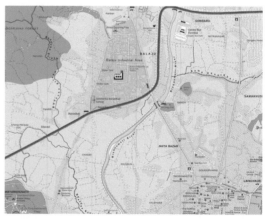

Figure 17: Road/tourist map

### 3-D MAP

3-D maps show a landscape in three dimensions (figure 18). They help us visualize an area as a continuous surface that rises and falls, showing the high and low values of the elevation.

Figure 18: 3-D map

### Use of maps

Maps give us a better understanding of a place. The information they contain depends on the type of map. However, maps are used to obtain answers to the following fundamental questions.

### LOCATION: WHERE ARE WE?

We sense our surroundings visually and attempt to locate ourselves with relation to visible features in our surroundings. We use rivers, mountains, buildings, trees, and other landmarks as references to where we stand. Similarly, we also think of places in terms of other places. For example, you know where you live relative to your friends' houses, your school, and the supermarket you visit.

Since these features are depicted on a map, with their positions relative to each other, we can locate ourselves by relating these features on the map and these features in our surroundings. To know exactly where we stand in a more scientific way, maps also provide information on latitude and longitude, the coordinate system to measure all places on the earth.

### NAVIGATION: WHERE ARE WE GOING?

Traveling is part of our daily life, whether it is going from our house to school or going from one city to another. Travel depends on skills of navigation; this is the ability to find a route from one place to another and back. Maps have been used as an aid for navigation since ancient times. From a tourist in a new town to the pilot of a fighter jet, everybody uses maps and navigation charts as a guide to reach to their destinations.

### INFORMATION: WHAT ELSE IS HERE?

Apart from road maps and topographic maps that help us locate ourselves and navigate, there are many other types of maps, which are made for conveying information on a specific topic. These are known as thematic maps. These maps are made for a purpose. Maps of rainfall, temperature, earthquake zones, household incomes, or spread of typhoid are thematic maps that give us information on a theme in the area concerned.

### EXPLORING: WHERE DO WE GO FROM HERE?

With developments in science and space technology, the making of maps and expansion of their uses has made great progress in the last few decades. Developments in data acquisition techniques—such as remote sensing, digital photogrammetry, and global positioning—and the graphic capabilities of computers have greatly changed mapping techniques and practices.

Mapping technologies are being used in many new applications. Biological researchers are exploring the molecular structure of DNA, or mapping the genome; geophysicists are mapping the structure of the earth's core; oceanographers are mapping the ocean floor; and so on. Mapping techniques are even being used to explore the relationships between ideas in what is known as concept mapping.

### MAP READING

Reading a map means interpreting colors, lines, and other symbols. Features are shown as points, lines, or areas, depending upon their size and extent (figure 19). Besides recognizing features, knowing their locations and relative distances is also important. Map symbols and map scale provide this information.

Figure 19: Types of map features

### POINT FEATURES

Point features, or geographically defined occurrences, are features whose location can be represented by a single x,y or x,y,z location. Points have no linear or area dimensions but simply define the location of a physical feature—control point monument, sign, utility pole—or an occurrence such as an accident.

### LINE FEATURES

Lines represent features that have a linear extent but no area dimensions. Centerlines of roads, water mains, and sewer mains are examples of line features.

### AREA FEATURES

Area features, also called polygons, have a defined two-dimensional extent and are delimited by boundary lines that encompass an area. Typical area features are maintenance districts and soil types.

### THREE-DIMENSIONAL SURFACES

Some geographic phenomena are best suited to representation in three dimensions. The most common example is surface terrain, often represented by contour lines that have an elevation value. This concept can be applied to other spatially continuous data as well. For instance, population density or income levels could be mapped as a third dimension to support demographic analysis or water consumption statistics.

### SCALE

Map scale describes the relationship between mapped size and actual size. It is expressed as a relationship between linear distances on the map and corresponding ground distance. Two methods of notating scale are commonly used.

Inch–foot equivalent: The scale relationship is expressed as 1 inch = × feet, in which the map distance of 1 inch equates to its corresponding ground distance.

Representative fraction (RF): This is a pure fraction that represents the ratio of map distance to ground distance without specifying any measurement unit. The inch–foot equivalent of 1 inch = 100 feet is represented in RF form as 1:1,200 or 1/1,200.

Large-scale maps cover small areas and usually include a greater level of detail than small-scale maps that depict larger areas in lesser detail. There are no precise definitions for large or small scale but, for most map users, the following general scale categories apply.

Large scale: 1" = 50' to 1" = 200'
(1:240 to 1:1,200)

Medium scale: 1" = 100' to 1" = 1,000'
(1:1,200 to 1:12,000)

Small scale: 1" = 1,000' to 1" = 5,000'
(1:6,000 to 1:60,000)

Very small scale: 1" = 5,000' and smaller
(1:60,000 and smaller)

## SYMBOLS

The meaning of each symbol used in a map is described in the map's legend. However, many symbols in topographic maps have become conventional and can be interpreted without looking at the legend. For example, an area feature shown in green is vegetation, blue is water, and a built-up area is gray or red. Similarly, many line symbols such as curved, dashed, dotted, or a combination are used to show various features. Usually the contours are brown, streams and canals are blue, roads are red and black, and borders are black dash-dots. Various point symbols are used to show schools, hospitals, temples, and so on. Figure 20 presents some of the standard symbology used in mapmaking.

Figure 20: Map symbols

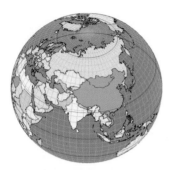

Figure 21: A globe

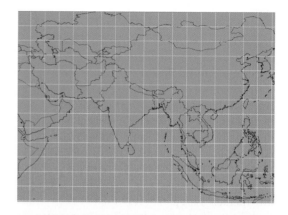

### MAP PROJECTION

A globe is the best way to show the relative positions of places, but it is neither portable nor practical for large scales (figure 21). The three-dimensional shape of the earth means that it is not possible to depict locations and features directly onto a two-dimensional map space without some distortions: try to flatten the skin of an orange onto a piece of paper. Map projection is a procedure that transforms locations and features from the three-dimensional surface of the earth onto two-dimensional paper in a defined and consistent way.

The transformation of map information from a sphere to a flat sheet can be accomplished in many ways. Mapmakers have invented projections that show distances, directions, shapes, or areas as they are on a globe to at least some extent. Each projection has advantages and disadvantages. Orthographic projections, for example, show shapes as they appear when the globe is viewed from space. Equal-area projections do not distort the size of areas but do distort their shape. Conformal projections are those on which the scale is the same in any direction at any point on the map. Many projections retain one geometric quality and a few retain more than one, but no single projection can accurately portray area, shape, scale, and direction (figures 22, 23, and 24).

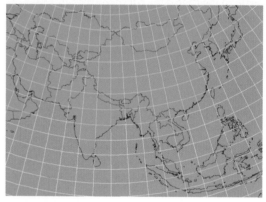

Figure 22: Plate carree projection and Albers equal area projection

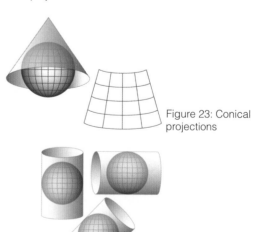

Figure 23: Conical projections

Figure 24: Cylindrical projections

# GIS

*"The new source of power is not money in the hands of a few but information in the hands of many."*

—John Naisbitt

Every day you wake at six o'clock in the morning. At eight o'clock you go to work, which is four kilometers south of your house. You return home at four o'clock in the afternoon, traveling along the same route. Then at five o'clock, you call your friends and arrange to have dinner at a restaurant that is a ten-minute walk from your house. Many of our activities are related to place and time in one way or the other. Planning and decision making—whether it is planning a new road or finding a suitable location for a health center—are influenced or dictated by location or a geographic component. The major challenges we face in the world today—overpopulation, deforestation, natural disasters—have a critical geographic dimension.

Our geography can be considered as a number of related data layers, as illustrated in figure 25. GIS combines layers of information about a place to give an understanding of that place. Which layers of information are combined depends on a purpose: for example, finding the best location for a new supermarket, assessing environmental damage, tracking delivery vehicles, or modeling the global environment. A GIS stores information about the world as a collection of thematic layers that can be linked together by geography. This simple, but extremely powerful and versatile concept has proven invaluable for solving many real-world problems.

In the strictest sense, a GIS is a computer system for collecting, storing, manipulating, and displaying geographic information. There are many definitions for GIS. However, its major characteristic is a geographic (spatial) analysis function that provides a means for deriving new information based on location.

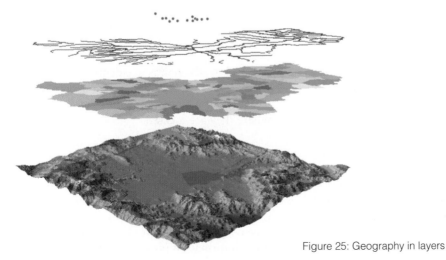

Figure 25: Geography in layers

*GIS functions*

There are four basic functions of a GIS: data capture, data management, spatial analysis, and presenting results.

### DATA CAPTURE

Data used in a GIS comes from many sources, is of many types, and is stored in different ways. A GIS provides tools and methods for the integration of data in formats that allow it to be compared and analyzed. Data sources are mainly manual digitization/scanning of aerial photographs, paper maps, and existing digital data. Remote-sensing satellite imagery and GPS are also data input sources.

### DATA MANAGEMENT

After data is collected and integrated, a GIS provides facilities that can contain and maintain data. Effective data management includes the following aspects: data security, data integrity, data storage and retrieval, and data maintenance.

### SPATIAL ANALYSIS

Spatial analysis is the most distinctive function of a GIS when compared to other systems such as computer-aided design (CAD). Spatial analysis includes such functions as spatial interpolation, buffering, and overlay operations.

### PRESENTING RESULTS

One of the most exciting aspects of a GIS is the variety of ways in which information can be presented once it has been processed. Traditional methods of tabulating and graphing data can be supplemented by maps and three-dimensional images. These capabilities have given rise to new fields such as exploratory cartography and scientific visualization. Visual presentation is one of the most remarkable capabilities of a GIS, which allows for effective communication of results.

*Questions GIS can answer*

A GIS can be distinguished by listing the types of questions it can answer.

### LOCATION: WHAT IS AT . . .?

This question seeks to find what exists at a particular location. A location can be described in many ways using, for example, a place name, postal code, or geographic reference such as longitude/latitude coordinates or x and y.

### CONDITION: WHERE IS IT . . .?

This question is the converse of the first and requires spatial data to answer. Instead of identifying what exists at a given location, one may wish to find locations where certain conditions are satisfied (e.g., a nonforested area of at least 2,000 square meters, within 100 meters of a road, and with soils suitable for supporting buildings).

### TRENDS: WHAT HAS CHANGED SINCE . . .?

This question might involve both of the first two and seeks to find the differences within an area over time (e.g., changes in forest cover or the extent of urbanization over the last ten years).

### PATTERNS: WHAT SPATIAL PATTERN EXISTS . . .?

This question is more sophisticated. It might be asked to determine whether landslides are occurring mostly near streams, or to find out at which traffic points accidents are occurring most frequently. It might be just as important to know how many anomalies there are and where they are located.

### MODELING: WHAT IF . . .?

This question is posed to determine what happens if, for example, a new road is added to a network or a toxic substance seeps into the local ground water supply. Answering this type of question requires both geographic and other information (as well as specific models).

*Geographic data*

There are two important components of geographic data: geographic position and attributes or properties—in other words, spatial data (where is it?) and attribute data (what is it?). Geographic position specifies the location of a feature or phenomenon by using a coordinate system. The attributes refer to the properties of spatial entities such as identity (e.g., maize, granite, lake), ordinal (e.g., ranking such as class 1, class 2, class 3), and scale (e.g., value such as water depth, elevation, erosion rate). These components are often referred to as nonspatial data since they do not in themselves represent location information.

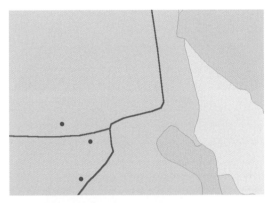

Figure 26: Vector format

## RASTER AND VECTOR DATA

Spatial features in a GIS database are stored in either vector or raster form. GIS data structures adhering to a vector format store the position of map features as pairs of x,y (and sometimes z) coordinates. A point is described by a single x,y coordinate pair and by its name or label. A line is described by a set of coordinate pairs and by its name or label. In theory, a line is described by an infinite number of points. In practice, this is of course not feasible. Therefore, a line is built up of straight line segments. An area, also called a polygon, is described by a set of coordinate pairs and by its name or label, with the difference that the coordinate pairs at the beginning and end are the same (figure 26).

A vector format represents the location and shape of features and boundaries precisely. Only the accuracy and scale of the map compilation process, the resolution of input devices, and the skill of the data-inputter limit precision.

In contrast, the raster or grid-based format generalizes map features as cells or pixels in a grid matrix (figure 27). The space is defined

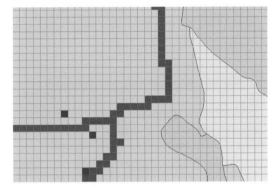

Figure 27: Raster format

by a matrix of points or cells organized into rows and columns. If the rows and columns are numbered, the position of each element can be specified by using column number and row number. These can be linked to coordinate positions through the introduction of a coordinate system. Each cell has an attribute value (a number) that represents a geographic phenomenon or nominal data such as land-use class, rainfall, or elevation. The fineness of the grid (in other words, the size of the cells in the grid matrix) will determine the level of detail in which map features can be represented. There are advantages to the raster format for storing and processing some types of data in a GIS. The vector–raster relationship is shown in figure 28.

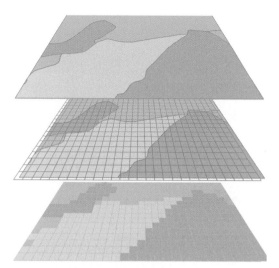

Figure 28: Vector–raster relationship

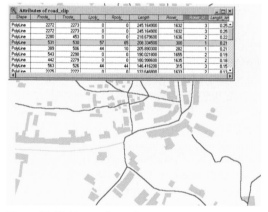

Figure 29: Linking attribute data

*Organizing attribute data*

A GIS uses raster and vector representations to model Earth features or phenomena. Apart from locations, a GIS must also record information about them. For example, the centerline that represents a road on a map does not tell you much about the road except its location. To determine the road's width or pavement type or condition, such information should be stored so that it can be accessed by the system as needed. This means that the GIS must provide a linkage between spatial and nonspatial data. These linkages make the GIS "intelligent," as the user can store and examine information about where things are and what they are like. The linkage between a map feature and its attributes is established by giving each feature at least one unique means of identification—a name or number, usually called its ID. Nonspatial attributes of the feature are then stored, usually in one or more separate files, under this ID number (figure 29).

This nonspatial data can be filed in several forms, depending on how it needs to be used and accessed. GIS software often uses a relational database management system (RDBMS) to handle attribute data.

A relational database organizes data as a series of tables that are logically associated with each other by shared attributes. Any data element in a relationship can be found by knowing the table name, the attribute (column) name, and the value of the primary key. The advantage of this system is that it is flexible and can answer any question formulated with logical and mathematical operators.

## Metadata

Metadata is simply defined as data about data. It gives the information about the content, source, quality, condition, and other relevant characteristics of the data (figure 30). For instance, it may describe the content as road or land-use data, the source as where the data has come from, the quality as the level of accuracy, the condition as whether the data is outdated or partial, and so on.

| ThemeName | Description | | Type | UniqueItem | Source | Scale |
|---|---|---|---|---|---|---|
| ROAD | Road network | | Shape: Arc | Road_ID | Topographic map | 1:25000 |

| SourceDate | Projection | Spheroid | Origin: | | FalseEasting: | FalseNorthing |
|---|---|---|---|---|---|---|
| 1995 | UTM | Everest | 84 00 00E, 26 15 00N | | 400000m | 0m |

| Xmin | Ymin | Xmax | Ymax |
|---|---|---|---|
| 714632.625 | 3028469 | 764657.625 | 3084497 |

**Covered Map Sheets**
2785-01d,02c,02d,03c,05b,06a,06b,07a,06d,06c,06d,07c,09b,10a,10b,10c

| Lookup Table/Description of Items | Quicklook Image |
|---|---|

| ROAD_ID | ROAD_TYPE |
|---|---|
| 1 | Highway |
| 2 | Major Road |
| 3 | Feeder Road |
| 4 | Foot Trails |
| 5 | Minor Foot Trails |

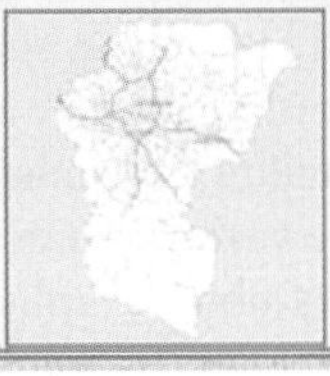

Figure 30: Metadata

# DATA CAPTURE

*"A decision is as good as the information that goes into it."*

—John F. Bookout, Jr.

*Data: the fuel*

Geographic data is information about the earth's surface and the objects found on it. Data is fuel to a GIS. How can we feed data such as a map into a GIS? Data capture is the process of putting information into the system. A wide variety of sources can be used for creating geographic data.

*Types and sources of geographic data*

Geographic data is generally available in two forms: analog data and digital data. Analog data is a physical product displaying information visually on paper, such as a map. Digital data is information that a computer can read, such as satellite transmissions.

There are various sources of digital data: maps, aerial photographs, satellite images, existing analog tables, and GPS receivers. Creating a database from such disparate sources (i.e., capturing the data) is the first and most time-consuming stage of a GIS project.

*Data capturing methods*

Methods of capturing data from various sources commonly used in a GIS are briefly discussed below.

PHOTOGRAMMETRIC COMPILATION

The primary source used in the process of photogrammetric compilation is aerial photography. Generally, the process involves using specialized equipment (a stereoplotter) to project overlapping aerial photos so that a viewer can see a three-dimensional picture of the terrain. This is known as a photogrammetric model. The current technological trend in photogrammetry is toward a greater use of digital procedures for map compilation.

DIGITIZING

A digitizing workstation with a digitizing tablet and cursor is typically used to trace digitize. Both the tablet and cursor are connected to a computer that controls their functions. Most digitizing tablets come in standard sizes that relate to engineering drawing sizes (A through E and larger). Digitizing involves tracing with a precise crosshair in the digitizing cursor features on a source map that is taped to the digitizing tablet, and instructing the computer to accept the location and type of the feature. The person performing the digitizing may input separate features into map layers or attach an attribute to identify the feature.

## MAP SCANNING

Optical scanning systems automatically capture map features, text, and symbols as individual cells or pixels and produce an automated product in raster format. Scanning outputs files in raster form, usually in one of several compressed formats to save storage space (e.g., TIFF, JPEG). Most scanning systems provide software to convert raster data to vector format that differentiates point, line, and area features. Scanning systems and software are becoming more sophisticated, with some ability to interpret symbols and text, and store this information in databases.

Creating an intelligent GIS database from a scanned map will require vectorizing the raster data and manual entry of attribute data from a scanned annotation.

## SATELLITE DATA

Earth resources satellites have become a source of huge amounts of data for GIS applications. The data obtained from satellites is in digital form and can be imported directly into a GIS. There are numerous satellite data sources such as LANDSAT or SPOT. A new generation of high-resolution satellite data, that will increase opportunities and options for GIS database development, is becoming available from private sources and national governments. These satellite systems will provide panchromatic (black and white) or multispectral data in the one- to three-meter range as compared to the ten- to thirty-meter range available from traditional remote-sensing satellites.

## FIELD DATA COLLECTION

Advances in hardware and software have greatly increased opportunities for capture of GIS data in the field (e.g., utility sign inventory, property surveys, land-use inventories).

In particular, electronic survey systems and the global positioning systems (GPS) have revolutionized surveying and field data collection. Electronic distance measurement services allow for survey data to be gathered quickly in an automated form for uploading to a GIS. Sophisticated GPS collection units provide a quick means of capturing the coordinates and attributes of features in the field.

## TABULAR DATA ENTRY

Some of the tabular attribute data that is normally in a GIS database exists on maps as annotation, or can be found in paper files. Information from these sources has to be converted to a digital form through keyboard entry. This kind of data entry is commonplace and relatively easy to accomplish.

## DOCUMENT SCANNING

Smaller format scanners can also be used to create raster files of documents such as permit forms, service cards, site photographs, and so on. These documents can be indexed in a relational database by number, type, date, engineering drawings, and so forth, and queried and displayed by users. GIS applications can be built that allow users to point to and retrieve for display a scanned document (e.g., tax parcel) interactively.

## TRANSLATION OF EXISTING DIGITAL DATA

Existing automated data may be available from existing tabular files maintained by outside sources. Many programs are available that perform this translation. In fact, there are many GIS packages with programs that translate data to and from several standard formats that are accepted widely by the mapping industry. They have been used as intermediate "exchange" formats for moving data between platforms (e.g., Intergraph® SIF, TIGER®, Shapefile, and AutoCAD® DXF™).

# REMOTE SENSING

*"To envision information—and what bright and splendid visions can result—is to work at the intersection of image, word, number, art."*

—Edward R. Tufte

## What is remote sensing?

We perceive the surrounding world through our five senses. Some senses (touch and taste) require contact of our sensing organs with the objects. However, we acquire much information about our surroundings through the senses of sight and hearing, which do not require close contact between the sensing organs and the external objects. In other words, we are performing remote sensing all the time.

Generally, remote sensing refers to the activities of recording/observing/perceiving (sensing) objects or events in distant (remote) places.

Remote sensing is defined as the science and technology by which the characteristics of objects of interest can be identified, measured, or analyzed without direct contact. Remote sensing deals with gathering information about the earth from a distance. This can be done a few meters from the earth's surface, from an aircraft flying hundreds or thousands of meters above the surface, or by a satellite orbiting hundreds of kilometers above the earth.

## Remote-sensing satellites

Remote-sensing satellites are equipped with sensors that look down at the earth. They are "eyes in the sky," constantly observing the earth (figure 32).

Figure 31: Earth from space

Figure 32: Remote-sensing satellite

## Why remote sensing?

Remote-sensing satellite images give a synoptic (bird's eye) view of any place on the earth's surface. This allows us to study, map, and monitor the earth's surface at local, regional, and global scales. It is cost effective and gives better spatial coverage compared to ground sampling.

*How does remote sensing work?*
Electromagnetic radiation reflected or emitted from an object is the usual source of remote-sensing data. A device to detect the electromagnetic radiation reflected or emitted is called a remote sensor. Cameras or scanners are examples of remote sensors. A vehicle to carry the sensor is called a platform. Aircraft or satellites are used as platforms.

The characteristics of an object can be determined using its reflected or emitted electromagnetic radiation. That is, each object has a unique characteristic of reflection or emission if the object type or environmental conditions are different. Remote sensing is a technology used to identify and understand the object or the environmental conditions through the uniqueness of its electromagnetic reflection or emission.

*Types of remote-sensing images*
Presently there are several remote-sensing satellite arrays in operation. Different satellite systems have different characteristics—such as resolution or number of bands on which they transmit—and have their own importance for different applications.

*Remote-sensing images*
Remote-sensing images are normally digital images (figure 33). In order to extract useful information, image processing techniques are applied to enhance the image to help visual interpretation, and to correct or restore the image if it has been subjected to geometric distortion, blurring, or degradation by other factors. There are many image analysis techniques available and the method used depends upon the requirements of the specific problem concerned.

Figure 33: Satellite images of Kathmandu

## USE OF REMOTE-SENSING DATA IN A GIS

Remote-sensing data can be integrated with other geographic data. There has been an increasing trend in the integration of remote-sensing data into a GIS for analytical purposes. There are many ways to use remote-sensing data; some examples are illustrated in figures 34 and 35.

Figure 34: Kathmandu urban area observed from an ADEOS-AVNIR M Japanese satellite image, 1997, and overlaid with road and river features

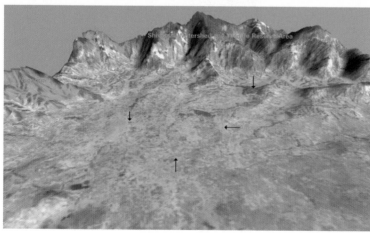

Figure 35: 3-D perspective of the Kathmandu valley generated by draping a LANDSAT-TM, 1998, satellite photo over a DEM

# GLOBAL POSITIONING SYSTEM

*"No matter where you go, there you are."*

—Anonymous

Knowing where you were and where you were going was the most crucial and challenging task faced by explorers in ancient times. Positioning and navigation are extremely important to many activities, and many tools and techniques have been adopted for this purpose. People have used a magnetic compass, sextant, or theodolite and measured the positions of the sun, moon, and stars to find their own position. More recently, a Global Positioning System (GPS) has been developed by the U.S. Department of Defense (DoD) for worldwide positioning at a cost of 12 billion U.S. dollars.

GPS is a worldwide radio-navigation system formed from a constellation of twenty-four satellites and five ground stations. It uses these "man-made stars" as reference points to calculate positions accurate to a matter of meters. GPS receivers are remarkably economical and have made the technology accessible to virtually everyone. The GPS provides continuous three-dimensional positioning twenty-four hours a day to military and civilian users throughout the world. These days, GPS is finding its way into cars, boats, planes, construction equipment, farm machinery, and even laptop computers. It has tremendous potential for use in GIS data collection, surveying, and mapping. GPS is increasingly used for precise positioning of geospatial data and collection of data in the field.

## Components of the GPS

The Global Positioning System is divided into three major components: the control segment, the space segment, and the user segment.

### CONTROL SEGMENT

The control segment consists of five monitoring stations—Colorado Springs, Ascension Island, Diego Garcia, Hawaii, and Kwajalein Island. Colorado Springs serves as the master control station. The control segment is the sole responsibility of the DoD, who undertakes the construction, launching, maintenance, and constant monitoring of all GPS satellites. The monitoring stations track all GPS signals and send correctional data back to the satellites.

The space segment consists of the constellation of Earth-orbiting satellites. The satellites are arrayed in six orbital planes inclined 55 degrees to the equator (figure 36). They orbit at an altitude of about 12,000 miles. Each satellite contains four precise atomic clocks (Rubidium and Cesium standards) and has a microprocessor on board for limited self-monitoring and data processing. The satellites are equipped with thrusters that can be used to maintain or modify their orbits, based on correctional data received from the tracking stations.

Figure 36: The satellites are deployed in a pattern that has each one passing over a monitoring station every twelve hours, with at least four visible in the sky at all times.

The user segment consists of all Earth-based GPS receivers. Receivers vary greatly in size and complexity, although the basic design is rather simple. The typical receiver is composed of an antenna and preamplifier, radio-signal microprocessor, control and display device, data recording unit, and power supply. The GPS receiver decodes the timing signals from the visible satellites (four or more) and, having calculated their distances, computes its own latitude, longitude, elevation, and time. This is a continuous process and generally the position is updated on a second-by-second basis. It is output to the receiver display device and, if the receiver provides data capture capabilities, stored by the receiver logging unit.

*How GPS works*

The GPS uses satellites and computers to calculate positions anywhere on Earth based on satellite ranging. This means that a position on Earth is determined by measuring its distance from a group of satellites in space. The GPS measures the time it takes for a radio message to travel from each satellite to the position on Earth. For this, it needs an extremely accurate clock. It then converts this time into a distance and, using triangulation, calculates each satellite's distance from Earth. It then needs to know where each satellite is in space. To compute a satellite's position in three dimensions, the GPS needs to have four satellite measurements. It uses a trigonometric approach to calculate these positions (figure 37). The satellites are so high that their orbits are very dependable.

## GPS errors

Although the GPS looks like a perfect system, there are a number of sources of errors that are difficult to eliminate.

### SATELLITE ERRORS

Slight inaccuracies in time-keeping by satellites can cause errors in calculating positions on Earth. Also, the satellite's position in space is important because it is used for the starting point of the calculations. Although GPS satellites are at extremely high orbits and are relatively free from the perturbing effects of atmosphere, they still drift slightly from their predicted orbits. Though they are regularly corrected, this drifting contributes to errors.

### THE ATMOSPHERE

The GPS signals have to travel through charged particles and water vapor in the atmosphere. This slows their transmission. Since the atmosphere varies in different places and times, it is not possible to compensate accurately for the delays that occur.

### MULTIPATH ERROR

As the GPS signal arrives on the Earth's surface, it may be reflected by local obstructions before it reaches the receiver's antenna. This is called multipath error because the signal reaches the antenna along multiple paths.

### RECEIVER ERROR

Receivers are also not perfect. They introduce errors that usually occur from their clocks or internal noise.

### SELECTIVE AVAILABILITY

Selective availability (S/A) was the intentional error introduced by the DoD to make sure that hostile forces could not use the accuracy of the GPS against the United States or its allies. Some noise was introduced into the GPS satellite clocks that reduced their accuracy. The satellites were also given erroneous orbital data that were transmitted as part of each satellite's status message. These two factors significantly reduced the accuracy of GPS for civilian uses. On May 1, 2000, the U.S. government announced a decision to discontinue the intentional degradation of public GPS signals. Civilian users of GPS are now able to pinpoint locations up to ten times more accurately. The decision to discontinue S/A is the latest measure in an ongoing effort to make GPS more responsive to civil and commercial uses worldwide.

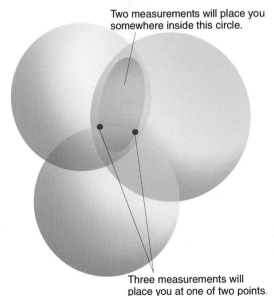

Two measurements will place you somewhere inside this circle.

Three measurements will place you at one of two points.

Figure 37: The first reading puts you somewhere on the globe. The second narrows the possibilities to the circle where the two globes intersect. The third places you at one of the two points (one of which can usually be disregarded).

*Differential positioning*

To eliminate most of the errors discussed above, the technique of differential positioning is applied. Differential GPS carries the triangulation principle one step further, with a second receiver at a known reference point. The reference station is placed on the control point—a triangulated position or the control-point coordinate. This allows for a correction factor to be calculated and applied to other roving GPS units used in the same area and in the same time series. This error correction allows for a considerable amount of error to be negated—potentially as much as 90 percent. The error correction can be made either by postprocessing or in real time (figure 38).

*Integration of GPS and GIS*

It is possible to integrate GPS positioning in GIS for field-data collection. GPS is also used in remote-sensing methods such as photogrammetry, aerial scanning, and video technology. GPS is an effective tool for GIS data capture. The GIS user community benefits from the use of GPS for locational data capture in various GIS applications. The GPS can easily be linked to a laptop computer in the field and, with appropriate software, users can place all their data on a common base with little distortion. Thus, GPS can help in several aspects of the construction of accurate and timely GIS databases.

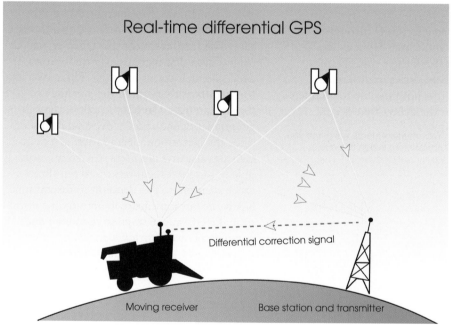

Figure 38: Differential positioning

## SPATIAL ANALYSIS

*"Knowing where things are and why is essential to rational decision making."*

—Jack Dangermond

When you think of a name and address database, you probably visualize a table of data in rows and columns. What you might miss is that each of these records represents a person or family that lives in a particular place (location). Furthermore, that particular location can tell us something about a person's standard of living, neighborhood, access to schools, access to a hospital, distance to the main market, vulnerability to local crime, exposure to pollution levels, and much more. GIS analysis allows us to visualize the "bigger picture" by allowing us to see patterns and relationships within the geographic data. The results of analysis may offer insight into a place, help focus actions, or select an appropriate option.

### What is spatial analysis?

Spatial analysis is a process for looking at geographic patterns in data and relationships between features. The actual methods used can be simple—just a map of the theme being analyzed—or more complex, involving models that mimic the world by combining many data layers.

Spatial analysis allows us to study real-world processes. It gives information about the real world that may be the present situation of specific areas and features, or changes and trends in a situation. For instance, it may be able to answer *where and by how much are forest areas decreasing or increasing?* or *where are urban areas growing in the Kathmandu valley?*

### Spatial analysis functions

Spatial analysis functions range from simple database query, to arithmetic and logical operation, to complicated model analysis. Each of these functions is briefly described below.

DATABASE QUERY

Database query is used to retrieve attribute data without altering the existing data. The function can be performed by simply clicking on the feature or by means of a conditional statement for complex queries. The conditional statement can involve Boolean (logical) operators—and, or, not, xor (exclusive of or)—or relational (conditional) operators— =, >, <, ≠ (not equal to). An example of Boolean operators that combine more than two conditions is shown in figure 39.

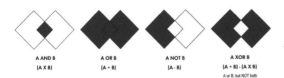

| A AND B | A OR B | A NOT B | A XOR B |
| (A X B) | (A + B) | (A - B) | (A + B) - (A X B) |
| | | | A or B, but NOT both |

Figure 39: Boolean operations

For example, in figure 40, the Boolean operator used is ([LandUse] = 'Agriculture') OR ([LandUse] = 'Shrub').

### RECLASSIFICATION

Reclassification operations involve the reassignment of thematic values to categories of an existing map. The following are examples.

- Classify an elevation map into classes with intervals of 500 meters (figure 41).
- Reclassify a VDC (village development committee) map based on population density (figure 42).

### OVERLAY

Overlay is at the core of GIS analysis operations. It combines several spatial features to generate new spatial elements. Overlay can be defined as a spatial operation that combines various geographic layers to generate new information. Overlay is done using arithmetic, Boolean, and relational operators, and is performed in both vector and raster domains.

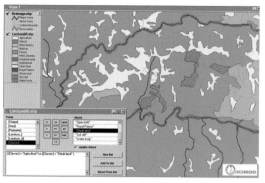

Figure 40: Selection using Boolean operators

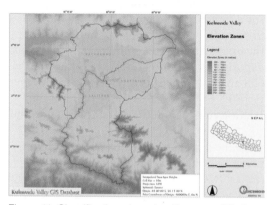

Figure 41: Classification of an elevation map of Kathmandu valley into different intervals

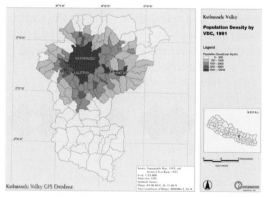

Figure 42: Classification of a VDC map of Kathmandu valley based on population density, 1991

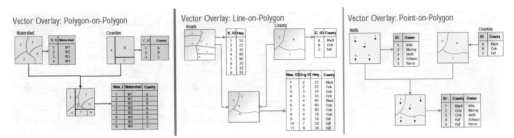

Figure 43: Vector overlay

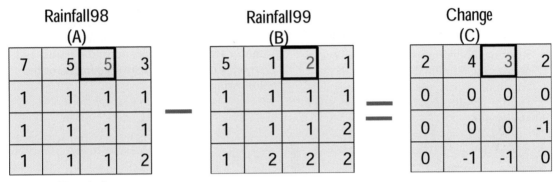

Figure 44: Map algebra

## Vector overlay

During vector overlay, map features and their associated attributes are integrated to produce a new composite map. Logical rules can be applied to determine how the maps are combined. Vector overlay can be performed on various types of map features: polygon-on-polygon, line-on-polygon, point-on-polygon (figure 43). During the process of overlay, the attribute data associated with each feature type are merged. The resulting table will contain all the attribute data.

## Raster overlay

In raster overlay, the pixel or grid cell values in each map are combined using arithmetic and Boolean operators to produce a new value in the composite map. The maps can be treated as arithmetic variables and perform complex algebraic functions. The method is often described as map algebra (figure 44). The map algebraic function uses mathematical expressions to create new raster layers by comparing them.

There are three groups of mathematical operators in the map calculator: arithmetic, Boolean, and relational.

- Arithmetic operators (+, −, ×, ÷) allow for the addition, subtraction, multiplication, and division of two raster maps or numbers or a combination of the two.

- Boolean operators (and, not, or, xor) use Boolean logic (true or false) on the input values. Output values of true are written as 1 and false as 0.

- Relational operators (<=, =, >, >=) evaluate specific relational conditions. If the condition is true, the output is assigned 1; if the condition is false, the output is assigned 0.

Figure 45 shows examples of simple raster overlay using different logical operators.

The following GIS application illustrates land-use and land-cover changes over time in the Kathmandu valley (figure 46). The analysis is done by overlaying land-use/land-cover data from different dates. The figure shows the land-use/land-cover data for 1978 and 1995, and the changes between 1978 and 1995 derived from this data.

This is the analysis of connectivity between points, lines, and polygons in terms of distance, area, travel time, optimum paths, and so on. Connectivity analysis consists of the following analyses.

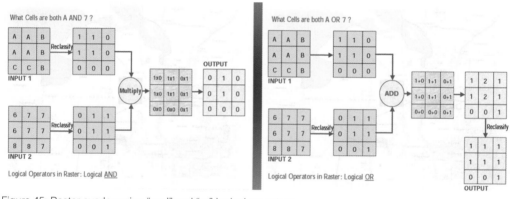

Figure 45: Raster overlay using "and" and "or" logical operators

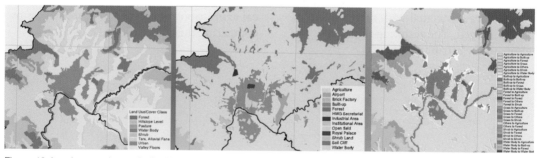

Figure 46: Land cover change in the Kathmandu valley between 1978 and 1995. The left panel shows land use/land cover of Kathmandu valley in 1978; the center panel shows the same in 1995. The right panel shows land use/land cover of the Kathmandu valley from 1978 to 1995.

## Proximity analysis

Proximity analysis is the measurement of distances from points, lines, and boundaries of polygons. One of the most popular types of proximity analysis is "buffering," by which a buffer zone with a given distance is generated around a point, line, or area, as shown in figure 47. Buffering is easier to generate for raster data than for vector data.

Figure 48 shows walking distances from the ICIMOD building.

## Network analysis

Network analysis is commonly used for analyzing the movement of resources from one location to another through a set of interconnected features. It includes determination of optimum paths using specified decision rules. The decision rules are likely to be based on criteria like minimum time or distance.

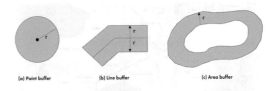

Figure 47: Buffer operations

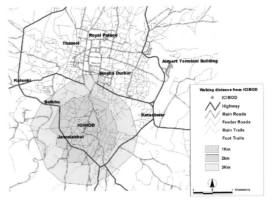

Figure 48: Walking distances from ICIMOD

# PRESENTING YOUR RESULTS

*"A picture is worth a thousand words."*

—Chinese proverb

### Visualization

Visualization is defined as the translation or conversion of spatial data from a database into graphics. These graphics are in the form of maps that enable the user to perceive the structure of the phenomenon or the area represented. The visualization process is guided by the question *How do I say what to whom, and is it effective? How* refers to the cartographic methods that are used for making the graphics or map. *I* refers to the cartographer or GIS user who is preparing the map. *Say* refers to the semantics that represent the spatial data. *What* refers to the spatial data and its characteristics, and the purpose of the map. *Whom* refers to the map's audience. The usefulness of a map depends upon the following factors.

### WHO IS GOING TO USE IT?

The map's audience or users will influence how a map should look. A map made for school children will be different from one made for scientists. Similarly, tourist maps and topographic maps of the same area are different in content and look as if they are made for different users.

### WHAT IS ITS PURPOSE?

The purpose of a map determines what features are included and how they are represented. Different purposes such as orientation and navigation, physical planning, management, and education lead to different categories of maps.

### WHAT IS ITS CONTENT?

A map's usefulness also depends upon its contents. Contents can be seen as primary content (main theme), secondary content (base-map information) and supporting content (legends, scale, and such).

### WHAT IS THE SCALE OF THE MAP?

The map scale is the ratio between a distance on a map and the corresponding distance in the terrain. Scale controls the amount of detail and extent of area that can be shown. Scale of the output map is based upon considerations such as the purpose of the map, needs of the map user, map content, size of the area mapped, accuracy required, and so on.

### WHAT IS THE PROJECTION OF THE MAP?

Every flat map of a curved surface is distorted. The choice of map projection determines how, where, and how much the map is distorted. Normally, map projections are chosen that correspond with the topographic maps that a particular country uses.

### HOW ACCURATE IS THE MAP?

GIS has simplified the process of information extraction and communication. Combining or integrating data sets has become possible. However, this has created the possibility of integrating irrelevant or inconsistent data. The user should be aware of aspects of data quality and accuracy. *What is the source of the data? Are the places at correct locations? Are the attribute values correct? Are the themes correctly labelled? Is the data complete?*

*Map design*

Mapmaking is both a science and an art. A beautiful map may be more popular than a plain map, even if it is less accurate. Maps influence people's perception of space. This influence is partly a result of convention and partly a result of the graphics used. People understand the world differently; they express this understanding differently in maps and also gain different understandings from maps.

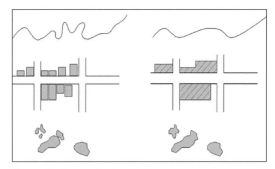
Figure 49: Generalization

GENERALIZATION

A map contains a certain level of detail depending on its scale and purpose. Large-scale maps usually contain more detail than small-scale maps. Cartographers often generalize the data by simplifying the information so that the map is easier to read (figure 49). The process of reducing the amount of detail on a map in a meaningful way is called generalization. Generalization is normally done when the map scale has to be reduced. However, the essence of the contents of the original map should be maintained. This implies maintaining geometric and attribute accuracy as well as the aesthetic quality of the map. There are two types of generalization—graphic and conceptual. Graphic generalization involves simplification, enlargement, displacement, or merging of geometric symbols. Conceptual generalization mainly deals with the attributes and requires knowledge of the map contents and the principles of the themes mapped.

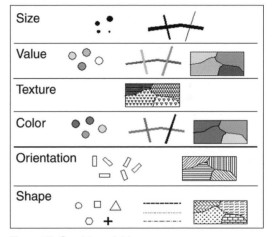
Figure 50: Graphic variables

GRAPHIC VARIABLES

Differences in the graphic character of symbols convey different perceptions to the map reader. These graphic characteristics are termed graphic variables and can be summarized as size, lightness or gray value, grain or texture, color, orientation, and shape or form (figure 50). Knowledge of graphic variables and their perceptual characteristics helps map designers to select those variables that provide a visualization that matches the data or the objective of the map.

Colors have psychological, physiological, and conventional aspects. It has been noted that it is difficult to perceive color in small areas, and greater contrast is perceived between some colors than others. In addition to distinguishing nominal categories, color differences are also used to show deviations or gradation.

Data needs to be analyzed before it is mapped. Data is either qualitative—roads, rivers, districts—or quantitative—elevation, temperature, population density. Representation also depends on the measurement scale used—nominal, ordinal, interval, or ratio scale.

For nominal scale, the differences in data are only of a qualitative nature (e.g., differences in gender, language, land use, or geology).

For ordinal scale, only the order of the attribute values is known and a hierarchy can be established such as *more than or less than; small, medium, large;* or *cool, tepid, hot.*

For interval scale, both the hierarchy and the exact difference are known but it is not possible to make a ratio between the measurements (e.g., temperature or altitude values). A temperature of 8 degrees C is not twice as warm as 4 degrees C; it is only the difference between two temperatures.

For ratio scale, data can be measured on a ratio measurement scale (e.g., the number of children in a family or an income).

Grouping of data can also be done in different ways. Ranges of values may be grouped according to natural breaks, at round numbers, at statistical means, or standard deviations. Different grouping or classification schemes give different perception of the phenomena.

*Mapping methods*
Mapping methods are standardized ways of applying graphic variables based on measurement scale and the nature of the distribution of objects. Various map types are given below.

Development regions of Nepal

Chorochromatic maps    This method renders nominal values for areas with different colors (in Greek, choros = area, chroma = color). The term is also used when patterns are used to render nominal area values. Only the nominal qualities are rendered and there is no suggestion of hierarchy or order conveyed.

Access to
safe drinking water

Major airports

**Choropleth maps** In this method, the values are rendered for areas (in Greek, choros = area, plethos = value). Values are calculated for area and expressed as stepped surfaces showing a series of discrete values. The differences in gray value or in intensity of a color denote the differences in the phenomenon. A hierarchy or order between the classes can be perceived.

**Nominal point data maps** Nominal data for point locations is represented by symbols that are different in shape, orientation, or color. Geometric or figurative symbols are more common in maps for tourists and schools.

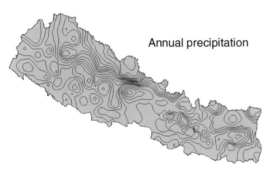

Annual precipitation

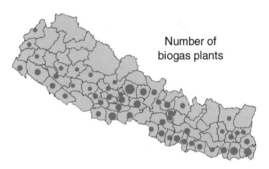

Number of
biogas plants

**Isoline maps** Isoline maps are based on the assumption that the phenomenon to be represented has a continuous distribution and smoothly changes in value in all directions of the plane. Isolines connect the points with an equal value (e.g., equal height above sea level or equal amounts of precipitation). Isoline maps show the trends of the phenomenon, such as in which direction it is increasing or decreasing.

**Absolute proportional maps** Discrete absolute values for points or areas are represented by proportional symbols. Different values are represented by symbols differing in size. The primary considerations for these symbols are legibility and comparability.

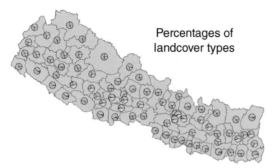

Percentages of landcover types

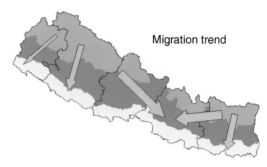

Migration trend

Diagram maps    Diagrams are used in maps to allow comparisons between figures or to visualize temporal trends. Line diagrams, bar graphs, histograms, or pie graphs are normally used on maps. However, care has to be taken that there are not so many distracting features that the image becomes too complicated.

Flowline maps    Flowline maps simulate movement using arrow symbols. Arrows indicate both route and direction of flows. The volume transported along the route is shown by the relative thickness of the arrow shaft.

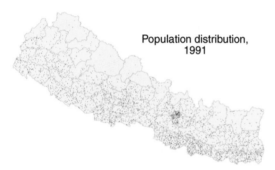

Population distribution, 1991

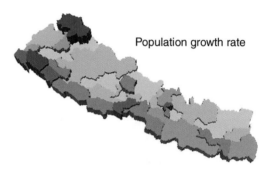

Population growth rate

Dot maps    Dot maps are a special case of proportional symbol maps, as they represent point data through symbols that each denote the same quantity, and that are located as closely as possible to the locations where the phenomenon occurs.

Statistical surfaces    Statistical surfaces are three-dimensional representations of qualitative data such as that used in choropleth and isoline maps.

## New map output types

New ways of visualization and using spatial information are being developed. New products such as electronic atlases, cartographic animations, and multimedia systems are appearing in the field of spatial information.

Multimedia allows for interactive integration of sound, animation, text, and video. In a GIS environment, this new technology offers a link to other kinds of information of geographic nature. These could be text documents describing a parcel, photographs of objects that exist in a GIS database, or a video clip of the landscape of the study area.

## Maps on the Internet

With new interactive tools and facilities offered by the Internet, maps are being used extensively online for various purposes. Apart from their traditional role of representing spatial data, maps can now function as an index of spatial data, a preview of data, and a search engine to locate spatial data. The Internet is becoming a major form of map distribution. With the new functions offered by map servers for interactive mapping, the user can define the content and design of maps. This is changing the way visualization applications are developed, delivered, and used.

Figure 51: Maps on the Internet (source: *www.mapquest.com*)

## IMPLEMENTING GIS

*"Few things are harder to put up with than the annoyance of a good example."*

—Mark Twain

GIS is an information management tool that helps us to store, organize, and use spatial information in a form that allows everyday tasks to be completed more efficiently. In the last two decades, GIS software, and the hardware required to operate it, has become much more affordable and easy to use. This means it's possible to develop a GIS without making large investments in software, hardware, and the support staff that were once needed to implement it. With the widespread implementation of GIS, we see dramatic improvements in the way we access information, execute responsibilities, and respond to requests from citizens, potential developers, and other clients.

*A working GIS*
A working GIS integrates five key components: hardware, software, data, people, and policy and procedures.

HARDWARE AND SOFTWARE
Hardware is the computer on which a GIS operates. Today, GIS software runs on a wide range of hardware types, from centralized computer servers to desktop computers used in stand-alone or networked configurations.

GIS software provides the functions and tools needed to store, analyze, and display geographic information. Key software components are as follows:

- Tools for the input and manipulation of geographic information
- A database management system (DBMS)
- Tools that support geographic query, analysis, and visualization
- A graphical user interface (GUI) for easy access to tools

The affordability of desktop computers with rapidly increasing power, and the decreasing cost of software has resulted in widespread use of desktop GIS.

## DATA

Data is one of the most important and costly components in implementing a GIS. The database is the longest existing part of any GIS implementation. Building the database takes the most time, costs the most money, and requires the most effort in terms of planning and management. Implementing a GIS requires adequate emphasis on database planning and choosing the right information base for the particular applications of an organization.

Most GIS applications in a particular area require a common set of spatial data. However, this data is often possessed by different organizations. A lack of adequate data-sharing mechanisms means that different organizations are involved in collecting the same data, wasting resources and time. This duplication of effort is also a result of insufficient or inappropriate standards in data collection. The major obstacle in the reuse of data is the lack of awareness or willingness among organizations to share data. GIS as a technology will only be viable and cost effective if data is readily available at an affordable cost.

## PEOPLE

GIS technology is of limited value without people to manage the system and develop plans for applying it to real-world problems. GIS users range from technical specialists, who design and maintain the system, to those who use it to help them perform their everyday work. GIS is a truly interdisciplinary field; it requires varied backgrounds of expertise, depending upon the applications. The skill all these people have in common is the ability to *think spatially*.

## POLICIES AND PROCEDURES

A successful GIS operates according to a well-designed plan and the business rules that are the models and operating practices unique to each organization. GIS exists in the context of application within an organization. The functional requirements of a municipal GIS are quite different from those of an agriculctural GIS, for example.

Besides technical components such as hardware, software, and databases, institutional frameworks and policies are also important for a functional GIS. The interest and willingness of decision makers to exploit GIS technology, and the organizational setup for collecting spatial data, analyzing it, and using the results for planning and implementation, form an important component of a GIS.

Choosing the right GIS for a particular implementation involves matching the GIS needs to the functionality demanded by the type of application required by an organization.

# GLOSSARY

## A

ablation   The loss of ice from a glacier as a result of melting and sublimation.

acid rain   Rainfall of more than usual acidity. Acid rain is believed to result largely from the human release of sulfur dioxide ($SO_2$) gas, especially from coal-fired electric generating plants.

acidification   Process by which soil or water become acidic.

aerial photograph   A photograph taken by a camera mounted on an airplane or balloon. Often used by cartographers as a base for other maps.

afforestation   Planting trees and plants.

Agenda 21   A document accepted by the participating nations at UNCED on a wide range of environmental and development issues.

AIDS   Acquired Immune Deficiency Syndrome: often fatal, infection is spread through sexual intercourse, blood transfusion, or sharing of hypodermic needles.

alien   Nonnative species introduced from another ecosystem.

amphibian   Living both on land and in water.

analog map   A map plotted on a permanent medium such as paper or transparent plastic sheets.

application   The use of software, data, procedures, and techniques in a series of steps that are then put into practice to solve a problem or perform a function. A computer program designed for a specific task or use.

aquifer   A porous and permeable layer of rock or sediment that contains large quantities of ground water and permits its ready movement.

atmosphere   Layers of air, composed of gases and particles, surrounding the earth.

## B

base map   A map portraying background reference information onto which other information is placed. Base maps usually show the location and extent of natural Earth surface features and permanent man-made objects.

Bilharzia   Tropical water-borne parasite, often called flatworm.

biodiversity   The variety of plants and animals that exist in nature, their interdependency, and the understanding that this web of connection is what sustains all life on the planet.

biogeography   The branch of geography concerned with the spatial characteristics of plants and animals.

biological pump   The process whereby carbon dioxide in the atmosphere is dissolved in seawater, where it is used for photosynthesis by phytoplankton, which are eaten by zooplankton.

biomass   A measure of vegetation density, defined as "the mass of vegetation per unit of area."

biome   A distinctive ecological system, characterized primarily by the nature of its vegetation.

biosphere   The region on land, in the oceans, and in the atmosphere inhabited by living organisms.

boundary   A line or set of lines defining the extent of an area having specific characteristics. A "logical" boundary is defined by human interpretation of geographical features (the boundary of ecosystems), while physical objects such as rivers, shorelines, and such define a "physical" boundary.

# C

cadastral map   A map showing the boundaries of the subdivisions of land for purposes of describing and recording ownership and/or taxation.

cadastre   A public register or survey that defines or re-establishes boundaries of public and private land for purposes of ownership and taxation.

carbon cycle   The exchange of carbon between the atmosphere, the land, and the seas.

carbon dioxide   One of the major greenhouse gases. Mainly the burning of fossil fuels and deforestation causes human-generated carbon dioxide.

cartographic enhancement   The addition of information to a map to make it easier to read, more descriptive of certain features, or simply to improve the way it looks.

cartographic models   A sequence of primitive spatial operations resulting in complex spatial models.

cartography   The science and art of making maps and charts.

CFCs   Chlorofluorocarbons: synthetic compounds used extensively for refrigeration and aerosol sprays until it was realized that they destroy ozone and have a very long lifetime once in the atmosphere.

CITES   Convention on International Trade in Endangered Species of flora and fauna.

climate   The long-term or overall condition of the atmosphere with respect to the weather elements and weather systems.

climate change   A significant alteration of long-standing weather patterns, attributed directly or indirectly to the consequences of human activity, above and beyond natural climate variability observed over comparable time periods.

climate system   The totality of the atmosphere, hydrosphere, biosphere, and geosphere, and their interactions.

composite map   A map on which the combined information from different thematic maps is presented. A composite may be created in the process of geographical analysis.

computer-aided drafting   A computer system that allows a person interactively to create and manipulate graphical data (i.e., points, lines, and polygons).

conservation   Preserving the environment.

consumption   The purchase and use of goods.

continuous map   A cartographic database that treats the entire mapped area as a single map, allowing the user to view any part of the map without opening a new file. This is in contrast to a database that breaks a mapped area into multiple files to minimize file size, just as a larger-scale paper map of a city is divided into multiple map sheets.

convention   An agreement between states or countries.

conversion   Translating data from one format into another. In a GIS most translation is from paper or transparent plastic maps into a digital spatial database.

coordinate geometry (COGO)   A set of procedures for encoding and manipulating bearings, distances, and angles of survey data into a graphic representation.

coppicing   The cropping of wood by judicious pruning so that the trees are not cut down entirely and can regrow.

crop yield   The amount of crops produced in a growing cycle.

# D

data dictionary   Indexes for databases, which describe data items, their formats, and their relationships with each other.

data model   An abstraction of the real world, which incorporates only those properties thought to be relevant to the application or applications at hand. The data model would normally define specific groups of entities, their attributes, and the relationships between these entities. A data model is independent of a computer system and its associated data structures. A map is one example of an analog data model.

database   An organized collection of information.

datum   Any point, line, or surface used as a reference for a measurement of another quantity.

deforestation   Clearing a forest of trees.

degradation   When the vitality or physical viability of a thing is worn away, reduced, or damaged.

derivative map   A map created by altering, combining, or analyzing other maps.

desertification   The expansion of deserts—related principally to poor agricultural practices, improper soil-moisture management, erosion and salinization, deforestation, and the ongoing climatic change—an unwanted semipermanent invasion into neighboring biomes.

digital elevation model (DEM)   A mathematical model that provides the data necessary to display the changing elevations of landforms. The term for the actual visual display itself.

digitize    The process of assigning digital coordinates by physically or automatically tracing hard-copy documents. Used for converting paper maps, aerial photos, or raster images into digital form.

digitizer    A device for entering the spatial coordinates of mapped features from a map or document to the computer.

# E

ecology    The science that studies the relations between organisms and their environment and among various ecosystems.

ecosystem    A distinct system of interdependent plants and animals, together with their physical environment.

edible landscaping    Planting trees and shrubs that produce fruits and vegetables.

El Niño    The anomalous warm ocean current that sometimes flows eastward across the southern Pacific to reach the coast of South America.

environment    All the factors determining the nature and existence of living organisms; includes physical, social, and cultural conditions that affect the development of that organism.

# F

food chain    The circuit along which energy flows from producers (plants), which manufacture their own food, to consumers (animals); a one-directional flow of chemical energy, ending with decomposers.

forest    An area in which trees are spaced sufficiently close together so that their foliage overlaps to form a more or less continuous canopy.

format    The way in which data is systematically arranged for transmission between computers, or between a computer and a device. Standard format systems are used for many purposes. The specified arrangement of data, such as the layout of a printed document, the arrangement of parts of computer instructions, or the arrangement of data in a record.

fossil fuels    Fuels such as coal, oil, and gas made by decomposition of ancient animal and plant remains which give off carbon dioxide when burned.

# G

geocoding    The process of assigning a geographic code to a record, event, or occurrence. For example, when using address processing software that equates an exact address with an address range related to a geographic code such as a ZIP Code, census tract, traffic zone, or municipal jurisdiction.

geodesy    The science which deals mathematically with the size and shape of the earth, with Earth's external gravity field, and with surveys of such precision that the overall size and shape of the earth must be taken into consideration.

geodetic datum    A datum consisting of five quantities: the latitude, longitude, and elevation above the reference spheroid of an initial point; a line from this point; and two constants which define the reference spheroid.

geographic information system (GIS)   A collection of computer hardware, software, and geographic data that captures, stores, updates, manipulates, analyzes, and displays all forms of geographically referenced information.

geography   The study of the world and all that is in it: its peoples; its land, air, and water; its plants and animals; and all the connections among its various parts.

global positioning system (GPS)   A space-based radio navigation system, consisting of twenty-four satellites and ground support that is owned and operated by the U.S. Department of Defense. The system provides users with accurate information about their position and velocity, the time anywhere in the world, as well as weather conditions.

global warming   The idea that increased greenhouse gases cause Earth's temperature to rise globally.

greenhouse effects   The heat-trapping ability of the atmosphere, especially of the gases carbon dioxide and water vapor.

greenhouse gasses   Those gaseous constituents of the atmosphere, both natural and anthropogenic, that absorb and re-emit infrared radiation.

ground water   Water that completely fills the pore spaces or other voids in the soil or rock below the water table.

# H

habitat   A physical location to which an organism is biologically suited. Most species have specific habitat parameters and limits.

# I

image processing   Computer techniques used to interpret and manipulate raster data and digitally remote sensed images.

incident map   A map that displays the location of an event (e.g., crime, accident, fire) used to identify spatial patterns or relationships with other geocoded data.

# J

jet stream   Relatively narrow bands of strong westerly winds centered in the upper troposphere above the middle latitudes and the subtropics of both hemispheres.

# L

landforms   Individual earth surface features.

layer   A logical separation of mapped information, according to theme. Many geographical information systems and CAD/CAM systems allow the user to choose and work on a single layer or any combination of layers at a time. A subset of digital map data, selected on a basis other than position. For example, one layer might consist of all features relating to roads, and another to buildings.

# M

map    A pictorial representation of the geographic location of selected surface features at a reduced scale.

map scale    The ratio of the distances between places on a map and those same distances on the earth's surface.

metadata    Data about data; for example, its source, accuracy, type, projection, and date of origination.

multipurpose cadastre    A comprehensive land information system at the parcel level. Land base includes all parcel boundaries, right-of-ways, and easements, with each parcel linked to supporting attribute records such as a survey control network land use, land cover, or political boundaries.

# N

National Spatial Data Infrastructure (NSDI) Coordinated by the Federal Geographic Data Committee (FGDC), the NSDI encompasses policies, standards, and procedures for organizations to cooperatively produce and share geographic data. The seventeen federal agencies that make up the FGDC are developing the NSDI in cooperation with organizations from state, local, and tribal governments; the academic community; and the private sector.

natural resource    Any element, material, or organism existing in nature that may be useful to humans.

natural vegetation    Plants that have been allowed to develop without obvious or significant interference from or modification by humans.

NGO    Nongovernmental organization.

nitrogen dioxide    A noxious reddish-brown gas produced in combustion engines; can be damaging to human respiratory tracts and to plants.

# O

orthophoto map    A photograph made from an assembly of orthophotographs. It may incorporate special cartographic treatment, photographic edge enhancement, color separation, or a combination of these.

orthophotograph    A photographic copy of an aerial perspective photograph, with distortions due to tilt and relief removed or corrected.

overlay    Information that is laid over or covers something else. In a manual graphic information system, a transparent sheet containing graphical data, such as labels, symbols, or colored areas, that is placed over another map to view spatial relationships. In an automated spatial information system, same as a manual system except that all overlays are in a digital format for viewing and interpretation on a cathode ray tube (CRT) screen. Each overlay defines a specific aspect of the spatial database.

oxidation    Chemical union of oxygen with other elements to form new chemical compounds.

ozone    Oxygen having three atoms of oxygen ($O_3$) forms a layer in the upper atmosphere that serves to screen out ultraviolet radiation harmful at Earth's surface.

ozonosphere    The region in the upper atmosphere where most atmospheric ozone is concentrated, from about eight to thirty miles above Earth, maximum ozone occurring at an altitude of about twelve miles.

# P

photogrammetry    The process of making measurements and maps or scaled drawings from photographs, especially aerial photographs.

photosynthesis    The synthesis of complex organic materials, especially carbohydrates, from carbon dioxide, water, and inorganic salts, using sunlight as the source of energy and with the aid of a catalyst, such as chlorophyll.

pollution    Alteration of the physical, chemical, or biological balance of the environment that has adverse effects on the normal functioning of all life forms.

preprocessing    In essence, preprocessing converts the measurement patterns to a form that allows a simplification in the decision rule. Preprocessing can bring patterns into congruence; remove noise; enhance images; segment target patterns; and detect, center, and normalize targets of interest.

projection    A mathematical method for representing the shape of the earth on a flat plane; a formula that converts latitude–longitude locations on the earth's spherical surface to x,y locations on a map's flat surface.

# R

radar    An instrument used to determine the approximate size, shape, and intensity of areas of precipitation. It emits pulses of microwave energy that are reflected from the precipitation and displayed on a screen.

radiation    The process in which energy is emitted as particles or waves.

raster    An image containing individual dots with color values, called cells (or pixels), arranged in a rectangular, evenly spaced array. Aerial photographs and satellite images are examples of raster images used in mapping.

rectification    A set of techniques for removing data errors through calculation or adjustment. In image processing, computer programs that remove distortion within a digital image, aerial photography, or remotely sensed data by removing parallax errors due to relief (high ground being closer to the camera than low-lying areas), camera tilt, awkward corners, and other distortions.

region    A geographic theme that focuses on areas that display unity and internal homogeneity or traits.

relief    Differences in elevation within an area. The topographic relief of a mapped area is computed by establishing and measuring the difference between its highest and lowest points.

remote sensing    Mechanical collection of information about the properties of an object or phenomenon using a recording device that is not in physical contact with the object of the study from a distance, usually from aircraft or spacecraft (e.g., photography, radar, or infrared).

renewable energy    Energy sources which are not depleted by use.

repeatability    The ability of a device to perform the same action consistently or to provide the same data given identical conditions. Given identical inputs, the limits within which the output will fall with a given statistical confidence.

respiration    The series of chemical reactions by which plants and animals break down stored foods with the use of oxygen, and consequently release energy, carbon dioxide, and water vapor.

# S

salinity    The concentration of natural elements and compounds dissolved in solution, as solutes, measured by weight in parts per thousand in seawater.

sanitation    Use of a network of pipes and treatment plants to drain and detoxify sewage and refuse.

scientific method    An approach that uses applied common sense in an organized and objective manner: based on observation, generalization, formulation of a hypothesis, testing, and the development of a theory.

soil erosion    The wearing away of topsoil by wind, rain, overcultivation, and so forth.

solar energy    Energy extracted from sunlight.

solid waste    Garbage, domestic, and industrial nondegradable waste materials.

spatial analysis    The examination of interactions, patterns, and variations over an area; an integrative approach to geography.

spatial data    Data that is inherently spatial in nature; a specific geographic location is associated with the individual data elements. It can be presented in one of three ways: as points, as vectors, or as polygons. It is sometimes used as a synonym for geometric data.

stereo plotter    A device for extracting information about the elevation of landforms from stereoscopic aerial photographs. The results are sets of x, y, and z coordinates.

stream digitizing    A method of digitizing from a map in which the cursor is drawn along a linear symbol, positions being recorded automatically at preset intervals of either distance or time. Contrasted with point digitizing.

structure query language (SQL)    A computer language for querying, updating, and managing relational databases.

sustainable development    Economic activity and other forms of social development that meet the needs of the present without compromising the ability of future generations to meet their own needs.

# T

topographic map    A map that portrays physical relief through the use of elevation contour lines that connect all points at the same elevation above or below a vertical datum, such as mean sea level.

topography    The combination of landform characteristics and distributions within a region.

topology    Based on a branch of mathematics called "graph theory," it deals with the relationships of simple geometries (i.e., points, lines, and polygons). These relationships can be used to automate and edit GIS data relating to both attributes and their graphic representations.

toponomy    The place names of a country, district, and so on, or the study of these.

transpiration    The transfer of water from plants to the atmosphere.

triangulated irregular network (TIN)    A presentation of a plane surface as a grid of triangular polygons. These models are used to represent elevations or other variables as a three-dimensional surface.

# U

UN    United Nations, headquartered in New York City.

UNCED    United Nations Conference on Environment and Development, held at Rio de Janeiro in June 1992, after which the United Nations Framework Convention on Climate Change was signed by 160 participating countries.

UNEP    United Nations Environment Programme, headquartered in Nairobi, Kenya.

urban heat island    Area of relatively warm temperatures associated with a city. The heat island results both from the nature of the city surface materials and from human activities that release heat.

urbanization    The building and growth of towns in rural areas.

UTM    The Universal Transverse Mercator grid system. In this orthogonal grid system, the earth from 84 degrees north to 80 degrees south latitude is divided up into many UTM zones. Each zone is 6 degrees east–west, and every grid square in every zone is of the same shape and size. UTM coordinate values are usually given in meters.

UV rays    Ultraviolet rays: an invisible form of energy harmful to most living organisms.

# V

vector    Any quantity having both amount and direction. Vectors are usually represented by directed line segments; the length of the line segment shows the vector quantity, and its direction is the same as that of the vector. A vector map contains the data about lines that allows the computer to calculate length and direction. This is contrasted with a raster map that displays images but not the data for line calculation.

vegetative succession    The gradual change in the composition of a plant community in response to changing environmental conditions following a disturbance such as a fire.

# W

**water table**   The upper boundary of the zone of permanently saturated soil or rock; the boundary between soil water and ground water.

**watershed**   The area drained by a river and its tributaries.

**wetland**   A narrow, vegetated strip occupying many coastal areas and estuaries worldwide; highly productive ecosystems with an ability to trap organic matter, nutrients, and sediment.

# BIBLIOGRAPHY

Bonham-Carter, Graeme F. 1994. *Geographic Information Systems for Geoscientists: Modeling with GIS*. New York: Pergamon/Elsevier Science Inc.

Christopherson, Robert W. 1997. *Geosystems: An Introduction to Physical Geography*, Third Edition. Upper Saddle River, New Jersey: Prentice Hall.

Committee on Planetary Biology. 1986. *Remote Sensing of the Biosphere*. Washington, D.C.: National Academy Press.

Eagles, Paul F. 1984. *The Planning and Management of Environmentally Sensitive Areas*. New York: Longman Inc.

Gabler, Robert E., Sheila M. Brazier, Robert J. Sager, and Daniel L. Wise. 1987. *Essentials of Physical Geography*, Third Edition. Philadelphia: Saunders College Publishing.

Harker, Donald F., and Elizabeth Ungar Natter. 1995. *Where We Live: A Citizen's Guide to Conducting a Community Environmental Inventory*. Washington, D.C.: Island Press.

Houghton, John. 1994. *Global Warming: The Complete Briefing*. Elgin, Illinois: Lion Publishing.

Lounsbury, John F., and Frank T. Aldrich. 1986. *Introduction to Geographic Field Methods and Techniques,* Second Edition. New York: Macmillan Publishing Company.

Scott, Ralph C. 1989. *Physical Geography*. Saint Paul, Minnesota: West Publishing Company.

United Nations Environment Programme and Peace Child International. 1999. *Pachamama: Our Earth,Our Future*. London: Evan Brothers, Ltd.

*A System for Survival: GIS and Sustainable Development*
Edited by Gary Amdahl
Editorial assistance by Claudia Naber
Book design, production, and image editing by Jennifer Johnston
Copyediting by Michael Hyatt and Tiffany Wilkerson
Cover design by Savitri Brant
Cartographic assistance by Edith M. Punt
Printing coordination by Cliff Crabbe